GREAT PRODUCT

Design

Distributor to the book trade in the
United States:

Publishing Group West
4065 Hollis Street
Emeryville, CA 94608

Distributor to the art trade in Canada:

Letraset Canada Limited,
and
Nielsen and Bainbridge
170 Duffield Drive
Markham, Ontario, L6G 1B5, Canada

Distributed throughout the rest of the
world by:

Hearst Books International
105 Madison Avenue
New York, NY 10016

Library of Congress Cataloging-in-Publication Data

Great product designs / by the editors of PBC International.
        p.   cm. -- (Library of applied design)
    Includes index.
    ISBN 0-86636-138-3
    1. Design, Industrial.   I. PBC International.   II. Series.
    TS171.G72   1990
    745.2--dc20   90-19298
                                                     CIP

Printing and binding by Toppan Printing
Co. (H.K.) Ltd.

PRINTED IN HONG KONG
10 9 8 7 6 5 4 3 2 1

GREAT PRODUCT
Design

The Library
of Applied
Design

An Imprint of PBC INTERNATIONAL Inc

CONTENTS

Introduction

What we work on is going to be ridden in, sat upon, looked at, talked into, activated, operated, or in some way used by people. . . . If the point of contact between the product and the people becomes a point of friction, then the industrial designer has failed. If people are made safer, more comfortable, more eager to purchase, more efficient—or just plain happier—the designer has succeeded.

—HENRY DREYFUSS
Designing for People

In approaching the formidable task of gathering material, we sought independent endorsement to help validate products for publication. With such a wide array of forms and functions, personal taste alone could not be authoritative. To begin with, we gathered products that had been recognized by recent international design competitions; these included the *ID Annual Design Review*, the Braun Prize, the ICSID/CID Philips Awards, Britain's Design Council Citations, the Osaka International Design Competition, and the Industrial Design Excellence Awards sponsored by the Industrial Designers Society of America. We also reviewed products that were selected for exhibition by galleries or museums; finally, the editors of *ID*, who are able to screen many new products, worked with Akiko Busch to select additional pieces by consensus.

The question of merit, of course, is always difficult; even when a jury is involved, subjective influences—such as aesthetics, fashion, taste, and the reputation of the designer, manufacturer, or retailer—come into play. Criteria vary, even within categories. In some cases, a product represents such an advanced and wonderful design solution that to include it seems absolutely right. In other instances, product differentiation is subtle and the reasons for inclusion obscure. Such disparate conditions are inevitable in any large collection.

In her lively and studious chapter introductions, Busch sets the stage for each of the ten chapters with relevant examples and an analysis of product design trends. In a collection as large as this one, however, we found it impossible to embark on a case-study approach, and to report the constraints and rationale that apply to each design.

One does not usually find careerist ambitions encapsulated in, say, a tape deck, but a designer *can* identify himself in the work; though there is no signature, the memory of the process can remain forever rich. In this sense, at the core of this collection is a tribute to the design process. As we recognize the elegant design of man-made objects, we recognize individual or collective imagination, intelligence, skill and talent.

What Ettore Sottsass, Jr., the Italian designer, said about a book on his work can be applied to this collection:

"A book is not real life: the daily grind, the anxiety, the confusion, the excuses of a headache or the radio that would not let you work in peace, the thousands of cards covered with sketches that seemed so brilliant because you never risked finishing them, and all those other distractions . . . in a finished book these things are no longer apparent."

The contemporary designer is the centerpiece of this collection, even where the design is anonymous. Though there are inevitable omissions, woven through the ten chapters is something of a who's who in contemporary international design.

The history of design since World War II reflects the uneasy coexistence of two distinct visions of the future, explains Jeffrey Meikle, author of *Twentieth Century Limited*. Both visions are illustrated in this collection; one, self-consciously elitist, stresses the moral, even the spiritual obligation of the designer, the other, more democratic, concentrates on providing the public with what it seems to want. In spite of this tension, designers are frequently able to please the critics *and* the public.

Even in this age of perpetual novelty, the level of mass design has improved; at the same time, *haut* design coexists with the Bauhaus ideal that "good" design can help reform society. In the everyday world, it may still be Raymond Loewy's MAYA axiom that is the most practical guide: it suggests that a designer should offer an inherently conservative public the "most advanced yet acceptable" version of a product.

Still another tension exists. There is the financial urge, based on economy of scale, to make products for the global market and the creative urge to produce for idiosyncratic segments that may or may not cross national boundaries. In the last ten years, product design has branched in many directions, pulled to and fro by competing artistic, financial, and marketing philosophies; the seamless modern aesthetic that guided design from the forties to the early seventies has been challenged by a healthy new diversity.

Design excellence does make a tangible contribution to a nation's economic well-being, according to author and economist John Kenneth Galbraith, the Paul Welberg Professor of Economics Emeritus at Harvard University.

". . . design depends not alone on the availability of artists, it invokes the whole depth and quality of the artistic tradition. It is on this that modern industrial success has come largely to depend. Proof is wonderfully evident. . . . One of the miracles of modern industrial development—of modern industrial achievement—has been modern Italy. Since World War II Italy has gone from one major public disaster to another with one of the highest rates of economic growth of any country in the Western industrial world. . . . Italy has been an economic success over the last 35 years because Italian design is better; because its products appeal more deeply to the artistic sense. An Italian design reflects . . . the superb commitment of Italy to artistic excellence extending over the centuries and continuing down to the present day."

There is also an evangelical side to *Product Design* in the sense that we want to help raise the level of design literacy. Though different from the way financial or marketing people think, the "designerly" way of thinking and communicating is vivid, and, in a world where old industrial patterns are fading, an approach to problem-solving that is increasingly relevant. Their combination of intuitive and logical thinking leads to true innovations, authentic product benefits, and elegant forms.

The traditional conflict between expedient marketing goals and design fidelity, has a powerful effect on the finished product. For example, a designer can be told, "Take out ten percent of the cost, but keep the perceived value." The compromise results in what is advertised as "style" and euphuistically called "cost-efficient design." In this common scenario, the designer tries to negotiate trade-offs in the consumer's favor, for it is the designer who is the custodian of the public's interest; in the vernacular, he represents the "end user."

The modern designer is expected to be familiar with aesthetics, engineering, ergonomics, fabrication, materials, marketing and sales. But in the practical world, success depends on team skills. When collaboration is sincere, it is exhilarating and leads to a high degree of design fidelity.

Yet design is never really anonymous, for refined products are made by companies that recognize aesthetic sensibilities, in short, the creativity of the individual. This is true whether the designer works for the corporation or is a member of an independent, consulting design firm. Because teamwork is inevitable, a culture of sensitive collaboration nourishes creativity.

CESHOUSEWARESTOOLSAPPLIANCESHOUSEWARESTOOLSAPPLIANCESHOUSEWARESTOOLSAPPLIANCESHOUSEWAREST
CESHOUSEWARESTOOLSAPPLIANCESHOUSEWARESTOOLSAPPLIANCESHOUS APPLIANCESHOUSEWAREST

CTRONICSENTERTAINMENTHOMEELECTRONICSENTERTAINMENTHOMEELE
INMENTHOMEELECTRONICSENTERTAINMENTHOMEELECTRONICSENTERTA

GLIGHTINGLIGHTINGLIGHTINGLIGHTINGLIGHTINGLIGHTINGLIGHTINGLIGHTINGLIGHTINGLIGHTING
GLIGHTINGLIGHTINGLIGHTINGLIGHTINGLIGHTINGL INGLIGHTINGLIGHTINGLIGHTINGLIGHTING

TRESIDENTIALFURNISHINGSCONTRACTRESIDENTIALFURNISHI
TIALFURNISHINGSCONTRACTRESIDENTIALFURNISHINGSCONTR

SEQUIPMENTBUSINESSEQUIPMENTBUSINESSEQUIPMENTBUSINESSEQUIPMENTBUSINESSEQUIPMENTBUSINESSEQU
SEQUIPMENTBUSINESSEQUIPMENTBUSINESSEQUIPMENTBUSINESS UI TBUSINESSEQU

EQUIPMENTMEDICALEQUIPMENTMEDICALEQUIPMENTMEDICALEQUIPMENTMED NTME
NTMEDICALEQUIPMENTMEDICALEQUIPMENTMEDICALEQUIPMENTMEDICALEQU ALEQ

IALEQUIPMENTTRANSPORTATIONINDUSTRIALEQUIPMENTTRANSPORTATIONINDUSTRIALEQUIPMENTTRANSPORTAT
IALEQUIPMENTTRANSPORTATIONINDUSTRIALEQUIPMENTTRANSPORTATIONINDUSTRIALEQUIPMENTTRANSPORTAT

IONALSPORTSEQUIPMENTRECREATIONALSPORTSEQUIPMENTRECREATIONALSPORTSEQUIPMENTRECREATIONALSPO
NTRECREATIONALSPORTSEQUIPMENTRECREATIONALSPORTSEQUIPMENTRECREATIONALSPORTSEQUIPMENTRECREA

STEXTILESTEXTILESTEXTILESTEXTILESTEXTILESTEXTILESTEXTILESTEXTILESTEXTILESTEXTILESTEXTILES
STEXTILESTEXTILESTEXTILESTEXTILESTEXTILESTEXTILESTEXTILESTEXTILESTEXTILESTEXTILESTEXTILES

FORTHEHANDICAPPEDDESIGNSFORTHEHANDICAPPEDDESIGNSFORTHEHANDICAPPEDDESIGNSFORTHEHANDICAPPED
ANDICAPPEDDESIGNSFORTHEHANDICAPPEDDESIGNSFORTHEHANDICAPPEDDESIGNSFORTHEHANDICAPPEDDESIGNS

Appliances Housewares and Tools

When industrial design first established itself as a field in the early days of this century, the products that emerged from the movement often resembled something else entirely. The consumer, in those days, may not have been entirely prepared for lamps, ice boxes, and radios that looked as though they did what they did. In fact, he or she generally preferred forms which, drawn from nature, were familiar. Witness, then, the streamlined iceboxes that appeared to be designed to travel at high speeds, lamps in the shape of dragonflies, and sewing machines gracefully lounging upon beds of ailanthus leaves.

All this, of course, changed with the Modern Movement, which measured the integrity of a form by the degree to which it expressed its function. For decades now, if any generalization could be made about home appliances, it is that their design had to clarify—beyond reasonable doubt—their function. Ailanthus leaves clearly obscured the issue of sewing. And, not only must an object look as though it does what it does, it should also simplify itself for the user. The uncluttered form found in most Braun classics perhaps best expresses this maxim.

While other areas of design may be staging minor revolutions that question these clean and classic lines of Modernism—most notably through a greater use of color and ornamentation—consumer appliances remain less playful. Form must continue to communicate function, not because its designers are unimaginative, but because the growing capabilities of consumer appliances make it all the more necessary for the shape of the object, the visibility of its graphics, and placement of controls all to contribute to the simplicity of operation and to make use self-evident. That is, few appliances have been able to afford to be ornamental without sacrificing some degree of clarity.

Still, no sooner are these words spoken than exceptions appear, and it is these exceptions that are one mark of contemporary design. The instant one passes swift judgment upon the overall purity of consumer appliances, products such as the Cyclon vacuum cleaner confront the eye. Described in one instance as "a successful mixture of a RCA degree show, Memphis, *Star Wars*, Art Deco, *Alien*, and Centre Pompidou styling motifs," it appears at first an anachronism. Indeed, ornamentalism is running rampant here. It shamelessly recollects the design by free association that marked the much earlier days of industrial design. The difference, though, is that the extravagant form of the machine celebrates, rather than conceals, its technical achievements. The purpose of the ailanthus leaves decorating the sewing machine was to suggest nature and thus diminish its possibly intimidating mechanical supremacy: By making the machine appear more "natural," they tried to make it more accessible, less intimidating. In the 1983 vacuum cleaner, the bizarre serves a different purpose: It glorifies the mechanism and flaunts technical innovation, which in this case is the application of centrifugal force to vacuum cleaner design.

It is this, then, that makes for much of the richness found in the design of many of these tools, appliances, and home products: While some quietly and eloquently express their function in simple, classical form, others, in their exuberance, are more likely to shout it.

But contemporary home appliances are distinguished by other features as well. In *A History of Industrial Design*, Edward Lucie Smith points out that the late nineteenth century kitchen could be regarded as a small factory that transformed raw materials into a finished product. While this was

certainly true then, it is also true now that the factory has become much smaller while the equipment intended for it has multiplied. In urban areas, especially, the kitchen is often no more than a narrow counter; meanwhile the array of its appliances and the special fixtures, features, and attachments intended for each are produced at a dizzying rate. So clearly, portability, miniaturization, and the ability of a product to file, fold, stack, stash, and perform any number of other reductive contortions to save space marks design excellence in the 1980s.

Or, given the fact that there still may not be enough space to store some of these items, their aesthetics must often be such that one does not mind seeing them even when they are not in use. An example is the prototype for a sculptural fire extinguisher. While its actual use is more likely to inspire terror, it remains a pleasure to look at.

It should perhaps be mentioned here that this and other prototypes have been presented here along with products that have been manufactured and marketed. The criteria used to judge this selection considered form and material more so than the test of the marketplace. While the latter is not insignificant and surely helps to ascertain the success of a product's design, its use as the single criterion for this selection would only exclude innovative and provocative design solutions that are yet in the conceptual or prototype stage.

Recent product design is distinguished as well simply for the range of categories in which it appears. With due thanks to Braun, we now expect calculators and hairdryers to be attentive to design. But screwdrivers and irons we do not. Industries not previously familiar with design have begun to showcase it. This indicates, perhaps, that competitive design work in product development may decide sales and that design entering new territories is another signpost of the 1980s.

If design in untraditional areas is one signpost, a parallel one is that traditionally "designed" products are being designed more and more frequently by professionals working outside the strict boundaries of

"industrial design." The silver teapots, for example, commissioned by Alessi, were designed by architects. Available for anywhere from $10,000 to $30,000, they are not exactly products to encourage serious consumer or manufacturer interest. Why, then, have they been included in a collection of product design? For the simple reason that invention can and often will come from without rather than within. Industrial designers can become so absorbed in the physics of material and process that they can bypass simple solutions. For this reason, it can be helpful to glance at the design solutions found elsewhere—solutions not of the economic use of material or process, for ones of pure form. There is a second reason as well: While these tea services may be prohibitively expensive, difficult to produce, and even more difficult to pour and drink from, they more successfully complete another part of their function. That is, they acknowledge and even celebrate the ritual of drinking tea. It is this less tangible function that can so easily be forgotten by the designer who designs housewares on a more regular and repetitive basis. What can designers of buildings say to designers of tableware? Can there be aesthetic cross references? While this selection does not necessarily try to answer these questions, asking that we consider them will surely only help to broaden our vision. And that it might promote a more collaborative spirit between the two professions justifies it all the more.

It also may be helpful to point out that there are absences in this broad category of products. Certainly, the items covered here have a wider range than those in any other category. Suitcases and wrenches, clocks and teapots are included. Still, freezers and dryers are not. It is not the aim here to represent the best of each appliance, but rather, by showing three well-designed vacuum cleaners, to show some of the ways in which it can be done, and by omitting freezers and dryers, to imply that they are areas that invite the designer's fine tuning.

Product:	Radius Two Collection
Designer:	William Sklaroff
	Philadelphia, Pennsylvania
Design Firm:	William Sklaroff Design Associates
	Philadelphia, Pennsylvania
Client:	Smith Metal Arts
	Buffalo, New York
Awards:	1981 IBD Product Design honorable
	mention
Materials:	In mirror brass, antique brass, mirror
	aluminum, mirror bronze, statuary
	bronze, or mirror black

Product: Safari Pens: Ball Point Pen, Mechanical
         Pencil, Inkwriter, and Fountain Pen
Designer: Wolfgang Fabian
         Heidelberg, West Germany
Client: C. Josef Lamy GmBH
         Heidelberg, West Germany
Materials: ABS plastic

Product: Lamy White Pens
Designer: Wolfgang Fabian
         Heidelberg, West Germany
Client: C. Josef Lamy GmBH
         Heidelberg, West Germany
Awards: Stuttgart Design Center award
         Hanover Gute Industrie Firm
Materials: White Makrolon casing, black
         polypropylene rings, black Delrin clip,
         and black Novodur cone

Product: Desk Accessories
Designers: Toru Nishioka and Studio 80
         Tokyo, Japan
Client: Courtesy Gallery 91
         New York, New York
Materials: Aluminum

Product:	Challenge Case and Briefcase
Design Firm:	Frogdesign
	Campbell, California
Client:	Louis Vuitton
	Paris, France
Materials:	Kevlar/polyurethane canvas; brass or chrome fittings, natural leather

Product: American Tourister Business Equipment
Designer: Ed Lawing, Richardson/Smith
Worthington, Ohio
Design Firm: Richardson/Smith
Worthington, Ohio
Client: American Tourister
Warren, Rhode Island
Materials: Injection-molded Lexan frame
with vacuum-formed shells
wrapped in top-grain cowhide

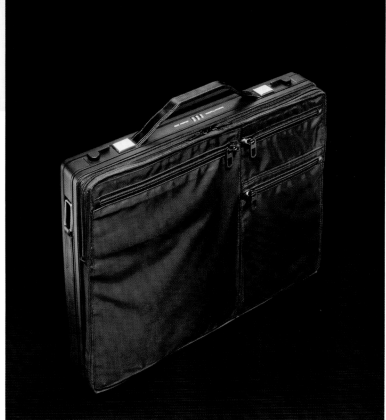

Product: Swedish attache case
Courtesy: Conran's
New York, New York
Materials: Pressed cardboard with black plastic
hardware

Product: Teapot with brass whistle sounding E and
              B notes
Designer: Richard Sapper
              Milan, Italy
Client: Alessi
              Milan, Italy
Courtesy: Sointu
              New York, New York
Materials: Stainless steel, heat diffusing copper
              bottom, polyamide covered handle

Product: Bistro tempered teapot and glasses
Courtesy: Conran's
              New York, New York
Materials: Glass, cork trivet, plastic details

Product: Tea and Coffee Service
Designer: Alessandro Mendini
Milan, Italy
Client: Alessi S.p.A
Milan, Italy
Materials: Silver

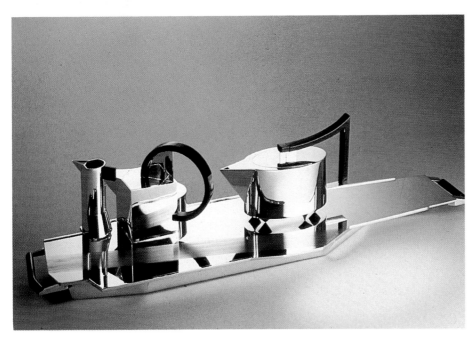

Product: Tea and Coffee Service
Designer: Hans Hollein
Vienna, Austria
Client: Alessi S.p.A.
Milan, Italy
Materials: Silver; knobs, handles, and feet in blue
metacrylate

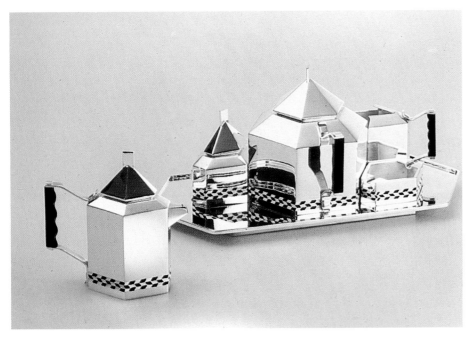

Product: Tea and Coffee Service
Designer: Paolo Portoghesi
Rome, Italy
Client: Alessi S.p.A.
Milan, Italy
Materials: Silver, ebony handles, decorative
enamelled black and white bands

Product: Reticelli
Designer: Michael Boehm
            Selb, West Germany
Client: Rosenthal Studio-Line, Rosenthal AG
            Selb, West Germany
Materials: Filigree glass

Product: Culinaria
Designers: Davin Stowell and Linda Celentano
              New York, New York
Design Firm: Davin Stowell Associates
              New York, New York
Client: Corning Designs
              Clinton, New Jersey
Materials: Pyrex and plated brass

Product: Marimekko for Pfaltzgraff Collection
Designer: Ristomatti Ratia
              Stamford, Connecticut
Client: Pfaltzgraff
              York, Pennsylvania
Materials: Stoneware

Product: Fruit Tray
Designer: Masanori Umeda
               Tokyo, Japan
Design Firm: Courtesy Gallery 91 New York, New York
Client: Courtesy Gallery 91 New York, New York
Materials: Aluminum

Product: Marimekko for Pfaltzgraff Collection
Designer: Ristomatti Ratia
             Stamford, Connecticut
Client: Pfaltzgraff
             York, Pennsylvania
Materials: Stoneware

Product: Frosted Champagne Flutes
Manufacturer: Hergiswiler Glaf AG
Hergiswil, Switzerland
Courtesy: Sointu
New York, New York
Materials: Frosted glass

Product: Tea and Coffee Service
Designer: Aldo Rossi
Venice, Italy
Client: Alessi S.p.A.
Milan, Italy
Materials: Silver; blue stoved enamel bands;
Storage unit: black iron base, glass
walls, brass frame.

Product: Executive Thermo Pitcher
Courtesy: Conran's
            New York, New York
Materials: Plastic with glass thermal liner

Product: Cruet Set
Designer: Ettore Sottsass
Milan, Italy
Client: Alessi
Milan, Italy
Courtesy: Sointu
New York, New York
Materials: Crystal with weighted bottoms; polished
stainless steel caps and tray

Product: Juice Jugs and Cups
Designer: Koen de Winter
Beaconsfield, Quebec, Canada
Client: Mepalservice
Lochem, The Netherlands
Awards: Selected for Design Collection of the
Museum of Modern Art in New York City
Materials: S.A.N.

Product: Domestic Sewing Machine
Designer: Roy S. W. Tam
            Essex, England
Awards: 1983 Braun Prize for Technical Design

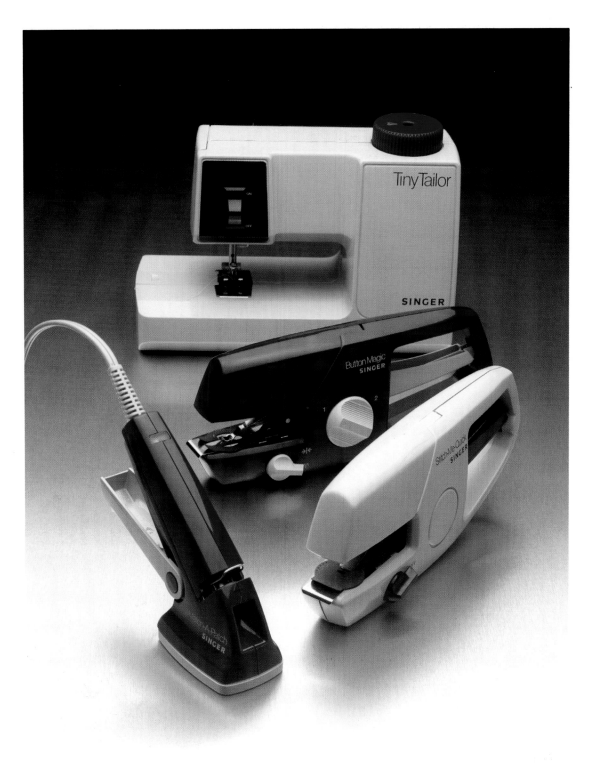

Product: Logica Electronic Sewing Machine
Designer: Giorgetto Giugiaro
              Moncalieri, Torino, Italy
Design Firm: Italdesign
              Moncalieri, Torino, Italy
Client: Necchi
              Pavia, Italy
Materials: Die-cast aluminum alloy, ephossidic
              resin electrostatic painted

Product: Singer Easy Menders: Tiny Tailor
              Mending machine, Button Magic Button
              Sewer, Stitch-Me-Quick Hem and Seam
              Mender, and Match-A-Patch Hole and
              Tear Mender
Designers: Michael Laude, Robert Dawson, Thomas
              Pendleton, and Andrew King Blance
              Casey Inc.
              New Canaan, Connecticut
Design Firm: King Casey Inc.
              New Canaan, Connecticut
Client: The Singer Company
              Stanford,Connecticut
Materials: Tiny Tailor; glass-filled thermo-set
              plastic; Button Magic Button Sewer and
              Stitch-Me-Quick Hem and Seam
              Mender: styrene and ABS; Match-A-
              Patch Hole and Tear Mender: ryton and
              polycarbonate

Product: CHRONOGYR room thermostat for small
              heating systems
Design Firm: Fellmann Design AG
              Dietlikon/ZH, Switzerland
Client: LGZ Landis & Gyr Zug AG
              Zug, Switzerland
Materials: Electronic circuit housed in gray-brown
              plastic

Product: Flip-top Durabeam
Design Firm: BIB Design Consultants
              London, England
Client: Duracell UK
              West Sussex, England
Materials: Black ABS plastic, yellow acetal
              moldings

Product: Allegroh
Design Firm: Frogdesign
Campbell, California
Client: Hansgrohe
West Germany
Awards: Stuttgart Design Center Excellence of
Design award
Materials: Steel ball, teflon covered joint

Product: Magazine Rack
Designer: Ann Maes
Eindoven, The Netherlands
Design Firm: Ann Maes Industrial Design
Eindoven, The Netherlands
Courtesy: Sointu
New York, New York
Materials: Steel with black enamel finish

Product: Dynamic Classics Auto Vacuum
Design Firm: Morrison S. Cousins and Associates
              New York, New York
Client: Dynamic Classics
              New York, New York
Awards: 1982 *Industrial Design* magazine Design
              Review selection
Materials: High-density polyethylene

Product:	Eureka Mighty Mite
Designer:	Kenneth R. Parker and Samuel E. Hohulin
	Bloomington, Illinois
Client:	The Eureka Company
	Bloomington, Illinois
Materials:	Injection molded ABS

Product:	Cyclon Vacuum Cleaner
Designer:	James Dyson
	Bath, England
Design Firm:	Prototypes
	Bath, England
Client:	Industrie Zanussie S.p.A.
	Pordenone, Italy
Materials:	ABS body, Macrolon polycarbonate, PVC hose, polyurethane hose cuffs

Product: Time of the Earth
Designer: Osamu Akiyama
Awards: 1st International Design Competition
            1983
            Osaka, Japan

Product: ETA 80 Telephone Set
Designer: Davorin Savnik
            Ljubljana, Yugoslavia
Client: ISKRA
            Ljubljana, Yugoslavia
Awards: 1981 Stuttgart Design Centre Award
            1980 Die Gute Industrieform, Hanover,
            West Germany
            8th Biennial of Industrial Design,
            Ljubljana, Yugoslavia
Materials: ABS plastic

Product: Vacform Wall Clock
Designer: Stephen Morgan
            London, England
Materials: Precolored polystyrene

Product: Braun Calculator
Designer: Dieter Rams
              Kronberg, West Germany
Client: Braun AG
              Kronberg, West Germany
Materials: ABS plastic

Product: Radius two Collection
Designer: William Sklaroff
              Philadelphia, Pennsylvania
Design Firm: William Sklaroff Design Associates
              Philadelphia, Pennsylvania
Client: Smith Metal Arts
              Buffalo, New York
Awards: 1981 IBD Product Design honorable
              mention
Materials: In mirror brass, antique brass, mirror
              aluminum, mirror bronze, statuary
              bronze, or mirror black

Product: Electric Drill
Design Firm: BIB Design Consultants
               London, England
Client: Black and Decker Ltd.
               Maidenhead, Berkshire, England

Product: Pocket Socket
Designers: Edward Levy and Michael Ballone
               Fort Lee, New Jersey
Design Firm: Innovations & Development, Inc.
               Fort Lee, New Jersey
Client: New Britain Tool Co., Div. of Litton
               Industries
               New Britain, Connecticut
Materials: Injection-molded ABS handle insert
               molded around die-cast chrome plated
               steel core; carrier for six sockets is
               injection-molded polypropylene.

Product:	Toro Compact 50 hose/reel system	Awards:	1980 *Industrial Design* magazine Design Review selection
Design Firm:	King Casey Inc. New Canaan, Connecticut		1980 IDSA Industrial Design Excellence Award
Client:	Toro Company Bloomington, Minnesota		Selected for permanent collection, Museum of Modern Art, New York, New York
		Materials:	ABS plastic; Hose: polyester fabric with bonded urethane loner; brass fittings

Home Electronics and Entertainment

The advent of electronics in home entertainment products has brought with it the attention of industrial designers. This does not come as any surprise—not only has the technology of electronics changed the size and shape of familiar products, but it has also generated the development of altogether new products. Both areas, clearly, are open invitations to the industrial designer.

To begin with, one of the most apparent features in contemporary consumer electronics is that they are smaller, lighter, more portable—and all the while, more durable. In terms of entertainment, at least, you *can* take it with you. And while their size and weight are diminished, so too is their price. Witness the range of new Sony products: the Walkman, Sport Walkman, and Music Shuttle all attest to the growing appeal of diminishing sizes. Likewise, the Watchman portable TV is 20 percent smaller and 20 percent lighter than its predecessor as a result of flat display picture tube technology.

Advanced electronics also give the consumer a wide range of product choices. Like most contemporary business products, the sophistication of home entertainment products is usually determined by the degree of control they offer the user. The Technics SL-QL15 turntable, for example, invites the user to "step into the world of programmable convenience" by selecting both the songs and the order in which they are to be played. An LED confirms the selection, and a repeat key will repeat the series. Songs within the program can also be skipped, repeated, or canceled in "random access programming" which is achieved by microcomputer technology. While this degree of programmable convenience may be necessary or convenient only to the very few, it is nevertheless what distinguishes "state of the art" consumer electronics.

Similarly, the ADS Atelier series of audio components offers a receiver which provides for connecting two tape decks and two sets of speakers, and allows the user to copy tapes while listening to the radio or playing a record. But the ADS series also demonstrates how the role of the designer is changing. Because electronics is itself such a recent product category, its design and manufacturing procedures have not yet become standardized. There is enough flexibility for the designer to have an integral role in actual product development, as indeed, in this case, Dieter Rams did. Collaborating with engineering specialists, Rams and the Braun electronics team were "responsible for helping conceive the various capabilities built into the products as well as extending these in a logical manner to the exterior envelope to ultimately contribute to accessibility and ease of use." That designers have recognized electronics as uncharted territory which invites and will accommodate their participation at much earlier stages benefits both their profession and engineering. More to the point, perhaps, is that the collaboration between the two signals a broader, more research-oriented approach to product development.

While this designer participation may result, in general, in a more integrated product, it may lead more particularly to a product that is human-engineered. The industrial designer is more likely than the engineer to consider how the user and the product will come to terms with one another. In Digital's Professional 350 personal computer, for example, the "human factors" research of the designers helped to specify at an early stage the angle of the tilt for the CRT, the angle for keyboard controls, mass storage access points, installation studies, cooling, internal component configurations, and cable management—as well as color, form, texture, material, manufacturing processes, and overall systems image—all the more traditional domain of the industrial designer. The system that evolved from this collaboration is indeed "an expandable system approach," which can accommodate a variety of personal computing capabilities, for telephone and database management to accessing to larger computing systems for executives and small businesses.

While the term "user-friendly" may have become somewhat stale, electronics engineers who continue to recognize the value of human factors input in the design of their equipment will continue to enjoy the edge. Despite their high visibility, electronics products remain unfamiliar— and, often, threatening enough to the general consumer that the convenient placement of their controls, absence of intimidating hardware, clear and informative graphics, and overall accessible appearance remain vital to their adoption and use. And as the capabilities of such equipment grow and become more complex, this will become all the more true.

By inviting designer participation at an earlier stage, particularly in new products, the electronics industry also introduces a whole new set of problems. The design of the compact disc player is a case in point. With the advent of digital audio recording, fidelity has reached a near perfect degree of accuracy. Digital audio is an outgrowth of computer technology which records, stores, and reproduces sounds by first giving them numerical codes. These codes are assigned to each "sample" of music being recorded, with samples taken 44,100 times each second. Digital signals engraved on a compact disc in the form of microscopic pits are then read by a laser beam (eliminating, of course, the need for the conventional needle, or stylus). The disc itself is only a little less than five inches in diameter.

What all this adds up to for the designer is that the new technology, aside from promoting miniaturization, also removes the traditional constraints of shape. Not only can the product be much smaller, but it doesn't necessarily need to be housed in the rectangular box of the traditional turntable and amplifier. Although this is certainly liberating to some degree, designers who "liberate" their products entirely from these conventions find themselves at a disadvantage. That is: the consumer looks for the familiar and searches out the recognizable. Even if the technology is brand new, if it *looks* brand new it is more than likely to put the consumer off. Products that look as though they do what they do—in the eyes of the

consumer—project a sense of logic which is reassuring. And new technology, when presented as such, can be intimidating. Thus, the design of digital audio equipment which takes conventional housing of audio equipment into account may meet with a better response than units which *look* as new as they really are. While ironies are implicit here, designers who recognize them—and the delicate balancing act they necessitate— perhaps achieve best results.

In concluding, it may be helpful to point out that some of the products shown here could have been shown as easily, or as appropriately, in other categories. The personal computers, most notably, are intended as much for use in small businesses as in the home. That several *are* included here only reiterates a point made elsewhere in this book—that as more and more people choose to work in their homes, equipment and furnishings for home and for office become less distinguishable. This is also why Richardson/Smith's 1982 computer prototype designed for *Time* magazine's "Machine [rather than Man] of the Year" is included here. As the computer becomes standard equipment for home as well as office, its design becomes more humanized. Hence the tilting and swiveling monitor, the adjustable, thin keyboard, and lively graphics that often serve more than one function. Designers for home electronics and entertainment products who note that the fine line between home and office is apt to become even finer are clearly recognizing their market.

If any overall conclusion is to be drawn from all this, it is that product design of this category demonstrates a more integrated, collaborative approach among designers, engineers, and technicians than in the past. Simply on account of its recent emergence, electronics and the development of electronic products have made room for the designer. Designers who have recognized this and responded by contributing to early product development are not only designing products that are as easy to operate as they are to look at; they are also setting new precedents for their colleagues working in other areas of design.

Product: JBL Auto Speakers
Designers: David Muramatsu, Tom Rupp, Luis
             Urquidi
             Orange, California
Design Firm: Halsted & Muramatsu, Orange,
             California
Client: JBL Sound, Northridge, California
Awards: 1983 *Industrial Design* magazine
             Design Review selection
Materials: Frame: brushed aluminum with black-
             epoxy metal powder paint coating; Logo:
             die-cast with JBL orange paint

Product: MCS Stereo Receiver 3285
Designers: Jan Tribbey and Rick Blanchard, JC
             Penney
             New York, New York
Client: JC Penney, New York, New York
Awards: 1983 *Industrial Design* magazine
             Design Review selection
Materials: Cabinet: vinyl-wrapped steel; facade:
             injection-molded ABS; control panel and
             switch caps: natural finish aluminum

Product: SL-QL15 Programmable Quartz Linear
              Tracking
              Turntable
Designer: Engineering staff, Matsushita Electrical
              and
              Industrial Company of Japan, Osaka,
              Japan
Client: Technics; Panasonic Company
              Division of Matsushita Electric
              Corporation of America
              Secaucus, New Jersey

Product: MCS Turntable 6730
Designers: Jan Tribbey and Rick Blanchard, JC
              Penney
              New York, New York
Client: JC Penney, New York, New York
Awards: 1983 *Industrial Design* magazine
              Design Review selection
Materials: Injection molded acrylic lens and dust
              cover; Feet: spring wrapped rubber;
              Base: injection molded acrylic and low-
              resonance foam; Control pads: injection
              molded ABS

Product: Concept 51 K
Design Firm: Frogdesign, Campbell, California
Client: Wega Electronic, West Germany
Materials: Polycarbonate housing

Product: MCS 1210 Stereo System
Designers: Jan Tribbey and Rick Blanchard, JC Penney;
Chris Hacker and Martin Thaler, Lee Manners and Associates, New York, New York
Client: JC Penney, New York, New York
Awards: 1983 *Industrial Design* magazine Design Review selection
Materials: Cabinets: particleboard with silver metallic vinyl wrap; Cabinet fronts: silver metallic injection-molded ABS; Speaker grilles: vacuum-formed ABS

Product: Apt 1 Stereo Power Amplifier
Designer: Charles Rozier, New York, New York
Client: Apt Corporation, Cambridge,
Massachusetts
Awards: 1981 *Industrial Design* magazine
Design Review selection
Materials: Formed steel case with gray wrinkle
finish enamel; painted aluminum front

Product: Kyocera DA-01 Compact Disc Player
Designer: Engineering division, Kyocera
International Inc.
Client: Kyocera International Inc., Warren, New
Jersey
Materials: Steel frame; Front panel: aluminum with
gunmetal finish; exterior wood panels

Product:	Beocenter 7700
Designer:	Design department, Bang & Olufsen A/S
	Struer, Denmark
Client:	Bang & Olufsen A/S, Struer, Denmark
Materials:	Injection molded chassis

Product: XRM-10 Music Shuttle
Designer: Sony Tokyo Design Engineers
Client: Sony Corporation, Tokyo, Japan

Product: ADS Atelier Audio Components
Designer: Dieter Rams
Clients: ADS, Analog & Digital Systems, Inc.,
Wilmington, Massachusetts,
and Braun Electronic GmbH
Kronberg, West Germany
Materials: Bevelled matte black components can be
stacked or set side by side

Product: FD-20A Watchman
Designer: Sony Tokyo Design Engineers
Client: Sony Corporation, Tokyo, Japan

Product: FD-30A Watchman
Designer: Sony Tokyo Design Engineers
Client: Sony Corporation, Tokyo, Japan

Product: Sony Sports Walkman
Designer: Sony Tokyo Design Engineers
Client: Sony Corporation, Tokyo, Japan

Product:	Steinberger Bass
Designer:	Ned Steinberger, Newburgh, New York
Client:	Steinberger Sound Corp., Staten Island, New York
Awards:	1981 IDSA Industrial Design Excellence Award
	1981 *Time* Magazine selection for five best of the year
Materials:	Neck and body: graphite-fiber and glass-fiber reinforced epoxy resin and polyester gel coat finish; solid brass and stainless steel hardware

Product: Seiko Pocket Color TV
Manufacturer: Seiko, Suwa Seikosha Co., Ltd., Suwa,
                Japan

Product: Microtek 36cm remote control portable
            television
Designers: H. Veaudry, M. A. Carr, C. Cunningham,
            and
            K. Chadwick and staff designers at
            Tek Electronics Ltd.
Client: Tek Electronics (pty) Limited
            Wilsonia, South Africa
Awards: 1982 Shell Design Award, consumer
            products
Materials: ABS housing

Product: FROGLINE Television Modules
Design Firm: frogdesign, Campbell, California
Client: Sony Corporation, Tokyo, Japan
Awards: Excellence of Design Award, Stuttgart
              Design Center
Materials: Polycarbonate and polystyrene

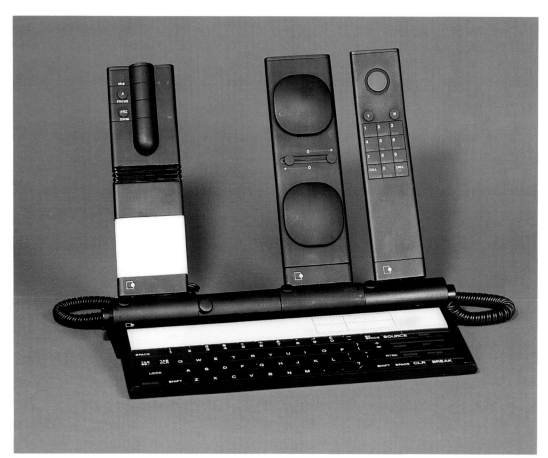

Product: Home computer prototype
Designer: Gustavo Rodriguez, Chicago, Illinois
Awards: 1983 Braun Prize for Technical Design

Product: IBM PCjr
Designer: IBM Entry Systems Division, Boca Raton, Florida
Client: IBM Corporation, Armonk, New York
Materials: Polycarbonate housing

Product:	Digital 350 Professional Series
Designer:	Industrial Design Group, Digital Equipment Maynard, Massachusetts
Client:	Digital Equipment, Maynard, Massachusetts
Awards:	1983 *Industrial Design* magazine Design Review selection
Materials:	All component housing injection molded in Noryl N-190; texture mold Tech 1013

Product:	Personal computer prototype designed to represent "The Machine of the Year" for *Time* magazine
Deisgner:	Ed Lawing, Richardson/Smith Worthington, Ohio
Design Firm:	Richardson/Smith, Worthington, Ohio
Client:	*Time* magazine, *Time*, Inc. New York, New York
Materials:	Acrylic and wood mockup

Lighting

For centuries people have been devising comfortable places to sit, convenient surfaces to put things on, and tools that will refine and extend their reach and capabilities. By design, we have made our world more accommodating. Not until much more recently, however, have we been able to enhance how we actually see the world. That is, not until the relatively recent discovery of electricity and the invention of artificial light.

Within this relatively recent history, lighting design has referred largely to the aesthetics of the fixture rather than to the actual quality of illumination. It is simply the short history, perhaps, that accounts for the narrow vision and definition of lighting design. But, for two reasons, lighting designers have finally come to consider the quality of illumination integral to lighting design. First is that recent and advanced lighting technology—most notably of enhanced fluorescents and tungsten-halogen lamps—has permitted and encouraged a discrimination in actual lighting sources as well as the lamps that house them. And second is the simple fact that seven-eighths of all our perceptions come through sight. With the available technology, designers can no longer afford to overlook, so to speak, how sight can be enhanced. So the current innovations in lighting are not necessarily an additional technology, but in the applications of existing technology.

American and European lighting designers have had two very different approaches to these applications. European designers have tended to determine the lighting requirements of a space before furnishing it. Americans, on the other hand, have been more prone to decide what needs to be lit before determining how it can be lit. Assuming that the light source, distribution, and placement of the lamp are the three foremost questions, they are ones most American designers feel cannot be answered until the natural daylighting and spatial relationships within the space have been determined. A fluorescent light, for example, will change the color of whatever it falls on, hence it would be foolish to decide to use a fluorescent lamp without knowing what, exactly, it was meant to light.

Nevertheless, this approach has all too often designated lighting as a secondary design element. It is from this deferential position that lighting designers have only recently begun to rescue their material. Architects and designers are beginning to accept notions well known to designers in the theater: Lighting affects mood and behavior; it can generate emotional and psychological responses ranging from apprehension and terror to tranquility and contentment. And although the office and home may be the backdrop for enactments usually less dramatic than those occurring on the stage, how these spaces are lit is surely as vital to the mood they finally project. Just as the socket and single bulb solution to lighting gave way to track lighting in the 1960s, the all-in-one, everything-at-once track fixture perhaps sacrificed the quality of illumination for convenience. It is now being replaced by more thoughtful applications that consider different lighting sources and purposes.

In determining the light source, the bearing of light upon color is perhaps most important. Incandescent lightbulbs produce a glow similar to that of afternoon sunlight: The light is the result of an object being heated to the degree at which it glows. Whether it comes from the sun or an electric bulb, the light has a continuous spectrum that begins at a warm red and shifts to a blue white as the heat intensifies. It is the richness in reds, however, that give

the bulb its warm red glow which appeals to most people because it enhances skin tone. Early fluorescent lights were deficient in reds, peaking instead in yellows and greens. Fluorescent lights now, however, have a much broader spectrum, more complete in blue and red areas and much closer to natural daylight. The light from some fluorescents now can resemble the warm reds of incandescents or late afternoon sunlight while the light emitted from others is closer to cooler, white midday light. Given the energy efficiency and practicality of fluorescents—long bulb life and diminished heat output—their increased application will perhaps have less to do with the quality of illumination they are able to achieve and more to do with putting aside traditional notions that fluorescent light is unnatural and thus unhealthy.

As much a variable as color is distribution: It can be direct, with 90 to 100 percent of its output downward; semidirect, with 40 to 60 percent of its output downward; diffused, with upward and downward output nearly equal; or indirect, with most of the light directed upward.

As designers become aware of the fact that lighting applications for home and office can have control and accuracy, they recognize the range of sources available to them and, indeed, lighting becomes a design element in its own right. The differences between incandescent and fluorescent lighting can highlight and dramatize one another: Because fluorescent light comes from a gas, it can appear to move and can be used in a dynamic composition with the more static light emitted from an incandescent. Or, artificial light can be selected to correspond to the natural daylighting of a space in a flexible—and energy efficient— arrangement that recognizes both time of day and time of year.

Tungsten-halogen lamps, often known as quartz, offer a new realm of possibilities. Although they are incandescent, they appear to produce more light from a smaller source. (Actually, it is just more

concentrated.) They also produce a slightly whiter light than the standard incandescent, and the bulb has a longer life.

If current lighting innovations are to be found in applications rather than new technology, no place presents a more imposing challenge than the electronic office. Especially with the ever present CRT screen, quantity of light becomes less of an issue than quality. The greatest problem is the standard recessed lighting found in most offices that exacerbates screen glare and creates distracting shadows on the keyboard. As lighting consultant James Nuckolls points out, "The distribution of specially designed assymetric task lights offered by several manufacturers were developed for flat paperwork; they added more glare than they prevented on the multipled angled surfaces of the CRT installations." Nuckolls continued to discover in preliminary studies that varied intensities were preferred to general illumination at one level. That is, copy stand, screen surface, background, keyboard area, and flat work area were best illuminated separately. He also found that cool tints of white light were preferred, that the light should come from above and slightly in front of the worker, and that the light on the background area was most effective when distributed unevenly. While these findings were preliminary, they do address the problems of eye strain and fatigue suffered by many CRT users. And, they reestablish the fact that the lighting requirements of the electronic workstation can be met by new applications rather than new technology.

Both the energy consciousness of the 1970s and the electronics of the 1980s have forced manufacturers and consumers to become innovative in searching out these new applications. As they continue to find them, lighting is apt to become a primary, rather than secondary, design element. Most conspicuous about contemporary lighting, perhaps, is that it is in this period of transition.

Product: BEGA Downlight
Design Firm: BEGA
              Menden, West Germany
Awards: iF Exhibition, "Good Industrial Design,"
              Hanover 1983
Materials: Aluminum alloy and stainless steel

Product: Aurora Borealis
Designer: Koen de Winter
             Beaconsfield, Quebec, Canada
Client: Danesco, Inc.
             Montreal, Quebec, Canada
Awards: 1982 Design Canada Award
Materials: Aluminum, baked epoxy

Product: Wall Lamp
Designers: King, Miranda, Arnaldi
             Milan, Italy
Client: Arteluce
             Milan, Italy
Awards: 1982 IBD Product Design Gold Award
Materials: Cast glass diffusor, metal wall bracket

Product: Aurora Borealis
Designer: Koen de Winter
            Beaconsfield, Quebec, Canada
Client: Danesco, Inc.
            Montreal, Quebec, Canada
Awards: 1982 Design Canada Award
Materials: Aluminum, baked epoxy

Product: Mary (single tube) and Mary Sue (double tube)
Design Firms: Walker/Group, Inc. and David A. Mintz, Inc.
New York, New York
Client: Lightron-of-Cornwall, Inc.
New Windsor, New York
Awards: 1983 IBD Product Design Gold Award
Materials: Cast aluminum steel wire grid, plastic refractor, fluorescent bulbs

Product: Lamps
Designer: Alvar Aalto (ca. 1940s and 1950s)
Reproduced
by: International Contract Furnishings
New York, New York
Materials: Painted brass and iron

Product: Aurora Borealis
Designer: Koen de Winter
Beaconsfield, Quebec, Canada
Client: Danesco, Inc.
Montreal, Quebec, Canada
Awards: 1982 Design Canada Award
Materials: Aluminum, baked epoxy

Product: Lamp (ca. 1952)
Designer: Alvar Aalto
Reproduced
by: International Contract Furnishings
New York, New York
Materials: Brass; inside painted white

Product: Cyclos
Designer: Michele de Lucchi
Milan, Italy
Client: Artemide Inc.
New York, New York
Materials: Gray painted metal structure with partial
frosted glass diffusor, fluorescent bulb

Product: Orbis
Designer: Ron Rezek
Los Angeles, California
Design Firm: Ron Rezek Lighting and Furniture
Los Angeles, California
Materials: Cast aluminum, brass, and stainless
steel

Product: Cabriolet
Designer: M. Coronelli and L. De Licio
Milan, Italy
Client: Thunder & Light/Stilnovo
Milan, Italy
Materials: Lacquered metal housing, opal squared
xerographied plexiglas, fluorescent
circular bulb

Product: Neon Sconce
Designer: Dan Chelsea and Rudi Stern of Let There
            Be Neon
            New York, New York
Client: George Kovacs Lighting, Inc.
            New York, New York
Materials: Black enamel, 100 watt halogen

Product: Tokio
Designer: Asahara Sigheaki
            Milan, Italy
Client: Thunder & Light/Stilnovo
            Milan, Italy
Materials: Makralon reflector and transformer-
            holder, lacquered metal supports,
            halogen bulb

Product: Lamps
Designer: Don Ruddy
               New York, New York
Design Firm: Furniture Club
               New York, New York
Materials: Concrete bases; ribbed, opaline acrylic
               diffusors; incandescent bulbs

Product: Lamps
Designer: Don Ruddy
               New York, New York
Design Firm: Furniture Club
               New York, New York
Materials: Concrete bases, rice paper between wire
               screening, incandescent bulbs

Product: Gibigiana
Designer: Achille Castiglioni
              Milan, Italy
Client: Flos of Italy
              Milan, Italy
Courtesy: Atelier International
              New York, New York
Awards: 1982 ASID International Product Design
              award
Materials: 20 watt halogen light source in
              cylindrical, form-bent metal base

Product: 110 Desk/Table Lamp
Designer: Ron Rezek
               Los Angeles, California
Design Firm: Ron Rezek Lighting and Furniture
               Los Angeles, California
Materials: Sheet metal, perforated steel reflector
               diffusor

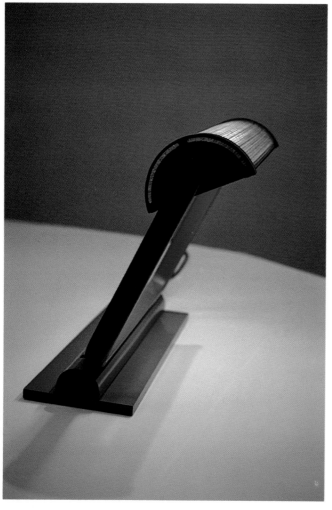

Product: Eubea Lamp
Designer: Alberto Fraser

Product: Sintesi Professional Task Lamp
Designer: Ernesto Gismondi
            Milan, Italy
Client: Artemide, Inc.
            New York, New York
Materials: Painted metal; diffusor cup in anodized
            aluminum with protective black metal
            grill

Product: Basic Lamp
Designer: John Willy Campbell
            West Yorkshire, England
Materials: Perforated steel and wood, 40 watt
            Roundlight Bayonet bulb

Product: Directional Lamp
Designer: John Willy Campbell
            West Yorkshire, England
Materials: Perforated steel and wood; 40 watt
            Roundlight Bayonet bulb.

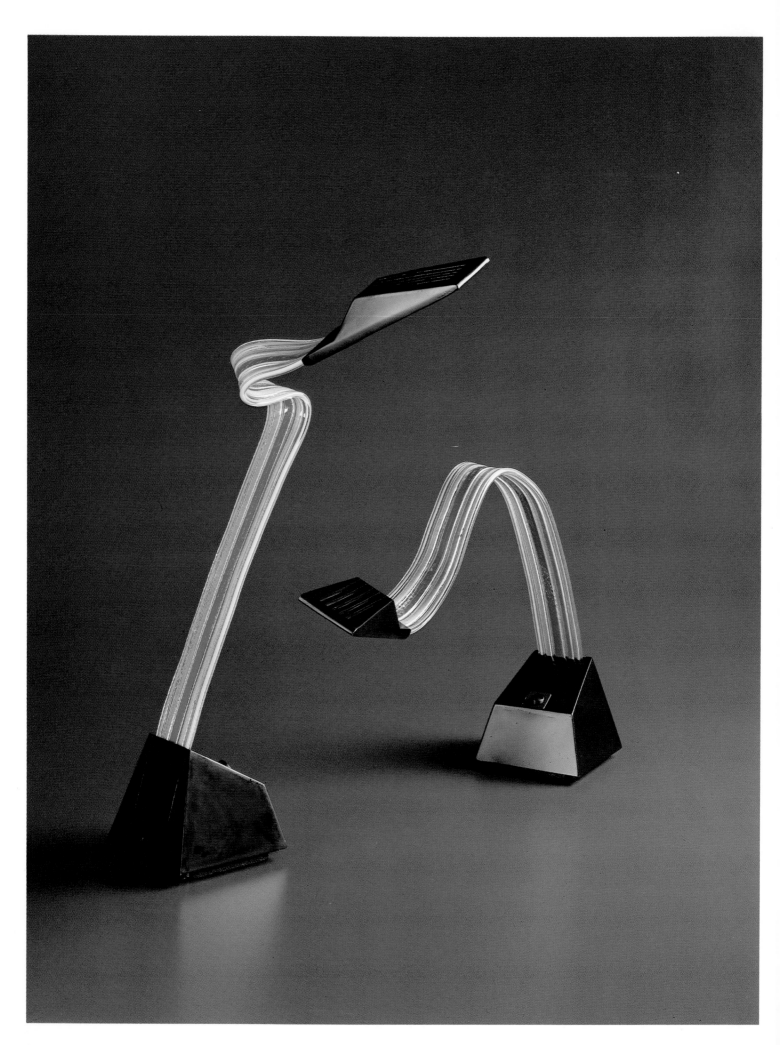

Product: Nastro Lamp
Designer: Alberto Fraser
Client: Stilnovo
            Milan, Italy
Materials: Halogen table lamp, multicolored plastic
            arm, transformer base and reflector,
            makrolon

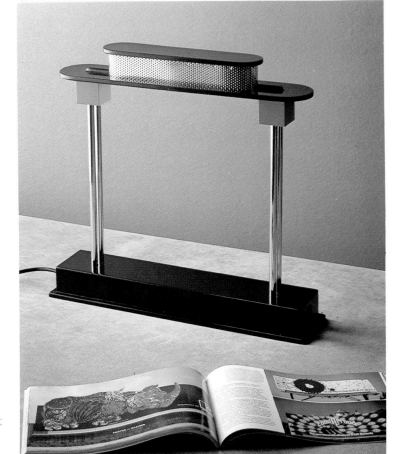

Product: Alistro
Designer: Ernesto Gismondi
            Milan, Italy
Client: Artemide Inc.
            New York, New York
Materials: Swivelling base in metal and molded
            glassfiber reinforced polyester:
            adjustable black metal arm; adjustable
            thermoplastic diffusor; fluorescent bulb

Product: Pausenia
Designer: Ettore Sottsass
            Milan, Italy
Client: Artemide Inc.
            New York, New York
Materials: Metal, polyurethane resin lacquer finish;
            chrome diffusor support columns;
            fluorescent bulb

Product: Lamps
Designer: Alvar Aalto (ca. 1940s and 1950s)
Reproduced
by: International Contract Furnishings
New York, New York
Materials: Painted brass and iron

Product: Aton Fluorescent
Designer: Ernesto Gismondi
Milan, Italy
Client: Artemide Inc.
New York, New York
Materials: Lacquered metal with metal base
encapsulated in black rubber coating;
Fluorescent

Product: Polifemo
Designer: Carlo Forcolini
             London, England
Client: Artemide Inc.
             New York, New York
Materials: Matte black metal, white lacquered metal
             reflector plate, halogen bulb

Product: Lamps
Designer: Alvar Aalto (ca. 1940s and 1950s)
Reproduced
by: International Contract Furnishings
             New York, New York
Materials: Painted brass and iron

Product: Neon Torch
Designer: Dan Chelsea and Rudi Stern of Let There
             Be Neon
             New York, New York
Client: George Kovacs Lighting, Inc.
             New York, New York
Materials: Anodized aluminum, 400 watt halogen
             with full range dimmer

Product: Catseye Emergency Standby Light
Designers: L. Eaton, A. Livermore, K. Gild, and staff
              design Durban, South Africa
Design Firm: Control Logic (Pty) Ltd.
              Durban, South Africa
Awards: 1982 Shell Design Consumer Product
              award
Materials: Extruded aluminum body, standard
              fluorescent tube

Product: Lighting Installation
Design Firm: Penney & Bernstein,
              New York, New York
Consultant
Firm: CHA Associates
              New York, New York
Client: Landor Associates
              New York, New York
Materials: Extruded aluminum channels with matte
              black nonreflective enamel finish; frame
              integrates wall and ceiling lighting with
              wiring and cable management systems;
              vertical lighting, tungsten-halogen wall
              washer; top component: tungsten-
              halogen indirect uplights

Contract and Residential Furnishings

In putting together a collection of contract and residential furnishings a number of questions are raised, the foremost of which is whether the two categories can be combined, or if it is more appropriate to treat them separately. The former course was chosen simply because so many of the products could have fallen into either category. An expansive mahogany table, for example, would be as suitable in a corporate conference room as in the dining area of a loft. Although office systems have yet to find applications in the home, and many of these pieces really can serve only in one area or the other, a great many others can adapt to either. What this signals, perhaps, is a shift in the way we perceive our homes and the places in which we work. While more and more people are devising ways in which they can work out of their homes, those who stay in the office appear to be looking for ways to make them look warmer and more comfortable—more, that is, like home. So it comes as no surprise that so many of these furnishings are serviceable in either place.

Another noticeable trend in recent furnishings is the homage much of it pays to history. Eileen Gray, Rennie Mackintosh, Le Corbusier, and a great many others have had their work reintroduced to the marketplace. While these designs, most now between 50 and 80 years old, are scarcely contemporary, they have been included in this chapter because they also represent current sensibilities. Whether it is for reasons of "vulgar commercialism" in the words of one designer, or a more thoughtful contemplation of form, designers are searching history for forms that may bear repetition. They are doing so in numbers high enough to indicate that it is neither aberrant nor anachronistic, but rather a substantive part of the way we view contemporary furnishings. Not to recognize this would also be failing to recognize the full scope of contemporary design sensibility.

What is also noticeable in this selection of furnishings is the number of pieces designed by architects. This is not exactly a novel idea. Most of the furniture in the Modern Movement was designed by architects who wanted the furnishings in a building's interior to correspond to the exterior form in its sense of proportion, attention to material and technological process, and the like. The inclusion of pieces designed by architects in this chapter, however, may need some justification. Although most of the furniture is conspicuous for its attention to form, material, and craft, it is less outstanding for its attention to the demands of production. Often, the designs are exercises in aesthetics that pay little heed to production costs, manufacturing processes, and the demands of the market. Still, these pieces are valuable reference points; often, it is the artist or designer working in one area of design who discovers what can be done in another. That designer, because he or she is less informed, may also have a less constrained vision of what possibilities exist. This is certainly not to say that industrial designers should look to architects for new ways to make tables, but simply that innovations can, and often do, come from outside a particular field. As often as an industrial designer designs a well-proportioned table that can be manufactured and marketed at a reasonable cost, an architect can come up with a form which, though it may be impractical, uses a refreshing color, has a whimsical curve, or uses a new laminate or building material that a designer more accustomed to making tables might not think to use.

What may signal these pieces most dramatically is their attention to—or captivation by—color and ornament. Though these elements may severely try the patience of any manufacturer adventuresome enough to take them on, the fact that they have entered the vocabulary of contemporary furnishings is enough in itself. Their message is implicit: Whether they go so far as to respond to "the need for our emotional participation in our environment" in the words of one Memphis advocate, or whether they are visual delights that are meant to give only pleasure, they attest finally that appearance need not reflect the pragmatc purpose of furniture.

They also ask that we shift our conventional attitudes toward furniture. Rather than look at a chair in terms of how it can be accommodated stylistically in a furnished room, or how it maintains some aesthetic continuity, these pieces ask that we accept them more individually. A chair, like a painting or ceramic vessel, can provoke, startle, and amaze as well as provide a place to sit.

Which brings us to the point of comfort. Many of the chairs included in this chapter, for example, rather shamelessly discourage the idea of sitting in them. Although this, at first, may seem to defeat the whole purpose of making a chair, it actually, on second thought, does not. What these designers seem to recognize is that although a great many chairs are indeed meant to be sat on, there are plenty of others which provide different services; while some chairs are meant to accommodate the human body as it works or eats, others wind up being a place to lace your shoes or hang a sweater. Since these chairs do not need to support the human frame for hours on end, they might as well look good doing what little they do.

If visual provocation rather than comfort marks much of what is new in residential furnishings, office systems pay all the closer attention to ergonomics. Witness the proportions of Neils Diffrient's Helena chair. The natural arc of the human body is nearly perfectly translated in the arc of the chair's back. Explains Diffrient: "Over the range of recline, you'll have a differential of only an eighth of an inch, which you won't even feel." The Helena Chair is only one example of these fine-tuned anthropometrics that acknowledge the need for office furniture to comfortably support the seated human frame for long stretches of time.

Another example is the Dorsal seating system by Emilio Ambasz and Giancarlo Piretti, which changes its configuration automatically whenever the user changes his or her position. Studies indicated that the frequent movement from a forward leaning position to a relaxed reclining position contributed to a healthy spine by encouraging the diffusion of nutrients in intervertebral disks. The backrest of the Dorsal seating system provides the user with support in any position, and thereby encourages this movement.

Ergonomics in the office, of course, is not limited to seating systems. Entire office systems can be—and are—designed to address ergonomics. In question particularly is how the office can sensibly integrate the rapid growth of electronic equipment with user need and comfort. The Activity Center Modules from Harvey Probber include glare-free laminated desk tops with adjustable height and tilt, acoustical privacy screens, and wire management ducts. The net effect is one of a personalized office space that accommodates individual postures and physiques, and adapts to diverse functions. Likewise, Ergodata by Precision Mfg. Co. is an office system which is based upon the integration of electronic data into the office. Again, wire and cable management channels and adjustable work surfaces are the keys that make it so flexible. While the ergonomics of designing a comfortable chair presents enough problems, designing a whole system geared toward both electronic equipment and its user is even more ambitious, and is perhaps what most distinguishes the office system of the 1980s. What this assures us, too, is that the whimsical attention paid to form in residential furnishings is balanced by the scrupulous attention to function found in office furnishings.

Product: Dunbar S/4 Series
Designers: Jack Dunbar, Lydia dePolo, and Steven
              Brooks
              New York, New York
Design firm: dePolo/Dunbar, New York, New York
Client: Dunbar, Berne, Indiana
Awards: 1982 IBD Product Design silver award
Materials: Reconstituted woods, plastic laminates,
              coordinated fabrics

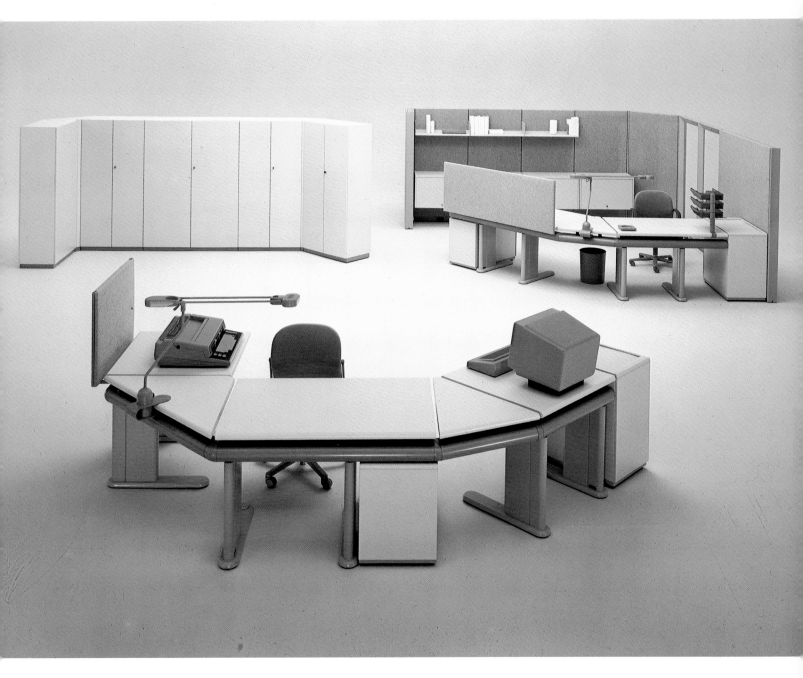

Product:	ACM ergonomically designed component system
Designer:	Karl Dittert, Giessen, West Germany
Client:	Probber/Voko, New York, New York
Awards:	1983 IBD Product Design silver award
	1983 Roscoe Product Design award
Materials:	Glare-free postformed laminate desk tops and steel desk bases

Product: Action Office
             Color, Fabric, Finish, and Texture System
Designer: Clino Castelli, Milan, Italy
Client: Herman Miller, Inc., Zeeland, Michigan
Materials: Include coordinated silkweaves, flannels,
             polyknits, perforated vinyls, and
             brushknits

Product: COM System (Continuum)
Designers: Francesco Frascaroli and C. Biondi,
             Bologna, Italy
Clients: C.O.M., Bologna, Italy
             Krueger, Inc., Green Bay, Wisconsin
Awards: 1983 IBD Product Design gold award
Materials: Legs: modular cast aluminum; Surfaces:
             high density particleboard with veneer or
             laminate finish; Connecting beams: steel

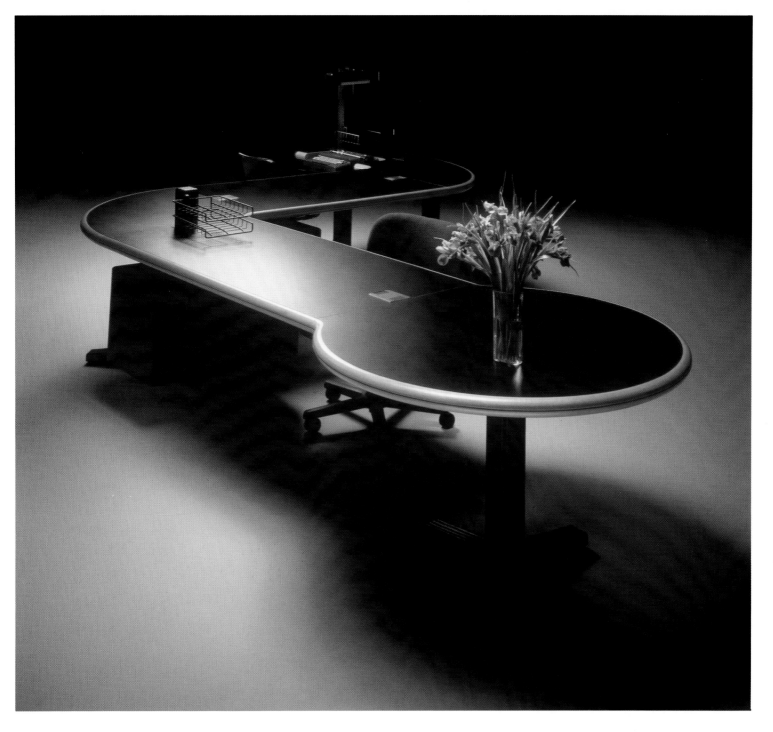

Product: COM System (Interval)
Designers: Francesco Frascaroli and C. Biondi,
             Bologna, Italy
Client: C.O.M., Bologna, Italy
             Krueger, Inc., Green Bay, Wisconsin
Awards: 1983 IBD Product Design gold award
Materials: Legs: modular cast aluminum; Surfaces:
             high density particleboard with veneer or
             laminate finish; Connecting beams: steel

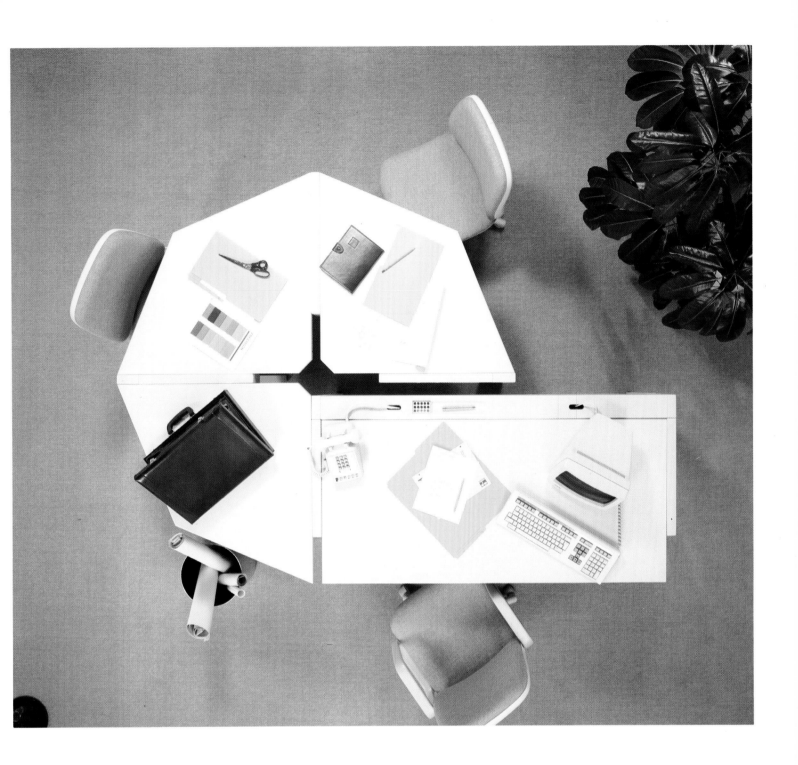

Product: Ergodata Office System with adjustable work
surfaces, acoustic panels, organizational channels
for power and communication cables

Designer: Urs Bachmann, Zurich, Switzerland

Client: Precision Manufacturing Company
Montreal, Quebec, Canada

Awards: 1983 IBD Product Design honorable mention

Materials: Surfaces: plastic laminate; Core: wood;
Frame: steel

Product: Data Entry Work Station
Designer: Bruce Hannah, Cold Spring, New York
Client: Knoll International, New York, New York
Materials: ABS plastic; steel frame; wood drawers

Product: Gwathmey Siegel Desk
Designer: Charles Gwathmey and Richard Siegel
New York, New York
Client: Knoll International, New York, New York
Materials: Drawers and compartment shelves: vinyl
covered fiberboard; hardwood drawer
pulls; Finishes: Techgrain or mahogany
veneer

Product: Desk and Drafting Table
Designer: Ron Rezek, Los Angeles, California
Design Firm: Ron Rezek Lighting + Furniture
Los Angeles, California
Awards: 1981 IBD Product Design gold award
Materials: Legs: heavy steel with plastic coating;
crossed tension cables and tubular
compression rods; Surfaces: Formica
Colorcore laminate

Product: Balans Activ 6000 and adjustable Activ
Working Table
Designer: Hans Chr. Mengshoel and Svein Gusrud,
Oslo, Norway
Client: HAG USA Inc., Chicago, Illinois
subsidiary of HAG A/F, Oslo, Norway
Materials: Frame: tubular stainless steel with
upholstered polyurethane cushions;
Tabletop: wood or plastic laminate

Product: Balans Vital 6035
Designer: Hans Chr. Mengshoel and Peter Opsvik,
Oslo, Norway
Client: HAG USA Inc., Chicago, Illinois
subsidiary of HAG A/F, Oslo, Norway
Materials: Base: aluminum; pneumatic lift; Seat:
foam/fabric covered plywood

Product: Stephens Office Seating/Management
            Chair
Designer: Bill Stephens, East Greenville,
            Pennsylvania
Client: Knoll International, New York, New York
Materials: Steel base; Finish: fused polyester;
            Upholstery: fabric, vinyl, or leather

Product: Stephens Office Seating/Executive Chair
Designer: Bill Stephens, East Greenville,
            Pennsylvania
Client: Knoll International, New York, New York
Materials: Steel base; Finish: fused polyester;
            Upholstery: fabric, vinyl, or leather

Product: Stephens Office Seating/Task Chair
Designer: Bill Stephens, East Greenville,
            Pennsylvania
Client: Knoll International, New York, New York
Materials: Steel base; Finish: fused polyester;
            Upholstery: fabric, vinyl, or leather

Product: Stephens Office Seating
Designer: Bill Stephens, East Greenville,
            Pennsylvania
Client: Knoll International, New York, New York
Materials: Steel base; Finish: fused polyester;
            Upholstery: fabric, vinyl, or leather

Product: Kevi™ Chair
(L-R): high-back management chair; sled base/pull-up chair; operational stool; secretarial chair; low-back management chair
Client: Herman Miller, Inc., Zeeland, Michigan
Materials: Shell: polystyrene; Armrests: polyurethane foam; Finish: polished aluminum or black umber epoxy base

Product: Dorsal™ Seating Range
Designer: Emilio Ambasz and Giancarlo Piretti New York, New York
Materials: Seats and backrests: injection molded thermoplastic; Hinge: steel with integral hinge mechanism; Legs: seam welded oval tubular steel components

Product: Flip-Seat™
Designer: David Goodwin, London, England
Design Firm: Goodwin-Wheeler Associates, London,
               England
Client: Fixtures Furniture, Kansas City, Missouri
Awards: 1983 IBD Product Design gold award
               1980 Design Council design Award
Materials: Seat: molded polypropylene; Frame:
               heavy gauge steel finished in epoxy

Product: Gina Chair
Designer: Bernd Makulik, Dudinghausen, West
              Germany
Client: Stendig International Inc., New York, New
              York
Awards: 1982 IBD Product Design gold award
              1982 Roscoe award
Materials: Frame: solid beech with fabric, vinyl, or
              leather upholstery

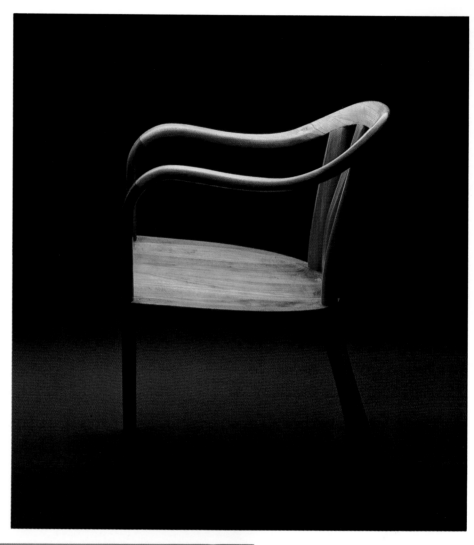

Product: Courthouse Chair
Designer: Walker/Group, Randy Stultz
              New York, New York
Design Firm: Walker/Group Inc., New York, New York
Client: The Gunlocke Company, Wayland, New
              York
Materials: Walnut

Product: Klassik & Klasse
Designer: Ernst Dettinger, Munich, West Germany
Client: Jack Lenor Larsen, New York, New York
Awards: 1981 Roscoe Product Design award
Materials: Solid beech

Product: Uni Chair
Designer: Werther Toffoloni, Udine, Italy
Client: Atelier International, New York, New York
Awards: 1983 *Industrial Design* magazine
             Design Review selection
Materials: Beechwood frame and legs; aluminum
             inserts secure legs to hardwood seat

Product: The Grid Chair
Designer: Ward Bennett, New York, New York
Design Firm: Ward Bennett Designs for Brickell
             Associates
             New York, New York
Materials: Kiln-dried solid ash with mahogany,
             natural oiled ash, black wax finishes and
             upholstered seat cushion

Product: Andover Chair
Designer: Davis Allen, New York, New York
Design Firm: Skidmore, Owings, and Merrill
             New York, New York
Client: Stendig International, Inc., New York,
             New York
Materials: Solid beechwood with fabric or leather
             upholstery

Product: Kita Collection
Designer: Toshiyuki Kita, Milan, Italy
Client: Stendig International Inc., New York, New
             York
Awards: 1983 IBD Product Design honorable
             mention
Materials: Beech and ash with matte polyurethane
             finish

Product: Willow 1 (1904), Hill House 1 (1902),
Argyle (1897)
Designer: Charles R. Mackintosh
Reproduced
by: Cassina of Italy, Milan, Italy
Materials: Willow 1: ebonized ashwood frame with
upholstered frame; Hill House 1:
ebonized ashwood frame with
upholstered frame; Argyle: ebonized
ashwood frame with upholstered frame

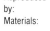

Product: LC 2 (1928)
Designer: Le Corbusier
Reproduced
by: Cassina of Italy, Milan, Italy
Materials: Frame: polished chrome plated or
enamel steel; Padding: polyurethane and
Dacron; Upholstery: fabric or leather

Product: D.S., 2–4 (1918)
Designer: Charles R. Mackinstosh
Reproduced
by: Cassina of Italy, Milan, Italy
Materials: Ebonized ashwood frame inlaid with
mother of pearl and sea grass seat

Product: Transat Armchair (1927)
Designer: Eileen Gray
Produced by: Ecart International, Paris, France
Distributed by: Furniture of the Twentieth Century Inc.
            New York, New York
Materials: Frame: lacquered wood; Details: nickel
            plated; Upholstery: black leather

Product: Willow 2 (1904)
Designer: Charles R. Mackintosh
Reproduced
by: Cassina of Italy, Milan, Italy
Materials: Ebonized ashwood frame inlaid with
             mother of pearl

Product: Zig-Zag (1934)
Designer: Gerrit T. Rietveld
Reproduced
by: Cassina of Italy, Milan, Italy
Materials: Unfinished or finished elm

Product: Red and Blue (1918)
Designer: Gerrit T. Rietveld
Reproduced
by: Cassina of Italy, Milan, Italy
Materials: Beechwood frame with lacquer finish on
             seat

Product: Lounge Chair (1929)
Designer: Rene Herbst
Produced by: Escart International, Paris, France
Distributed by: Furniture of the Twentieth Century, Inc.
                 New York, New York
Materials: Finish: Nickel-plated steel or semi-matte
                 black

Product: Inna
Designer: Pennti Hakala, Helsinki, Finland
Client: Inno, Inno-tuote Oy, Helsinki, Finland
Materials: Plywood seat; linen cloth; canvas or
            leather cushions

Product: Carlos Riart Chair
Designer: Carlos Riart, Barcelona, Spain
Client: Knoll International, New York, New York
Awards: 1983 Roscoe Product Design award
Materials: Ebony with Brazilian amaranthe with
             mother-of-pearl inlays or holly wood with
             ebony inlays

Product: Slim Chair
Designer: Johan Huldt, Sweden
Client: Conran's, New York, New York
Materials: Removable cotton cover on tubular steel
            frame and polypropelene sling

Product: Botta Chair
Designer: Mario Botta, Lugano, Switzerland
Client: ICF, New York, New York
Materials: Frame: steel tubing with silver or black
epoxy; Seat: perforated steel with silver
or black epoxy; Back: self-skinned
expanded charcoal polyurethane

Product: Steamer Collection
Designer: Thomas Lamb, Uxbridge, Ontario,
Canada
Client: Ambiant Systems Ltd., Toronto, Ontario,
Canada
Awards: Permanent Design Study Collection of
the
Museum of Modern Art
1982 Roscoe Award
1983 IBD Product Design gold award
Materials: Veneer: Canadian maple coated in clear
lacquer or black stain

Product: Conference Table
Designers: Shane Kennedy and Don Ruddy, New York, New York
Design Firm: Furniture Club, New York, New York
Materials: Top: cinder-gray concrete; Legs: sulphur yellow concrete

Product: Coffee table
Designer: Shane Kennedy and Don Ruddy, New York, New York
Design Firm: Furniture Club, New York, New York
Materials: Legs: terra cotta; Top: glass

Product: Pina Gamba
Designer: Geoffrey Frost, Topanga, California
Design Firm: Frost Design, Topanga, California
Awards: 1983 IBD Product Design silver award
Materials: Concrete and glass

Product: Adjustable-height table
Designers: Keith Muller, Anne Carlyle, Mark Campbell
Toronto, Ontario, Canada
Design Firm: Keith Muller Limited
Toronto, Ontario, Canada/Washington D.C., USA
Client: Alberta Children's Hospital
Calgary, Alberta, Canada
Materials: Tabletop: plastic laminate with one-inch hardwood edge; Base: brushed aluminum; gas cylinder in central supporting column adjusts height of table

Product: Lucia Mercer Collection
Designer: Lucia Mercer, Vermont
Client: Knoll International, New York, New York
Materials: Granite

Product:	Hospital bedside table
Designers:	Keith Muller, Anne Carlyle, Mark Campbell
	Toronto, Ontario, Canada
Design Firm:	Keith Muller Limited
	Toronto, Ontario, Canada/Washington, D.C., USA
Client:	Alberta Children's Hospital
	Calgary, Alberta, Canada
Awards:	1983 *Industrial Design* magazine Design Review selection
Materials:	Wood with natural finish; plastic tray top

Product: Temple Chair
Designers: Jim Lewis and Clark Ellefson
Columbus, South Carolina
Design Firm: Lewis & Clark, Columbus, South
Carolina
Designed for: Colorcore™ "Surface & Ornament"
Competition I and Exhibition
Awards: "Surface & Ornament" Competition, 1st
Prize winner
Materials: Colorcore™ surfacing material by
Formica Corporation

Product: Strata
Designer: Brian Faucheux, Metairie, Louisiana
Designed for: Colorcore™ "Surface & Ornament"
Competition I and Exhibition
Awards: "Surface & Ornament" Competition, 3rd
Prize Winner
Materials: Colorcore™ surfacing material by
Formica Corporation

Product: Neapolitan
Designer: Lee Payne, Atlanta, Georgia
Design Firm: Lee Payne Associates, Inc., Atlanta, Georgia
Designed for: Colorcore™ "Surface & Ornament" Competition I and Exhibition
Awards: "Surface & Ornament" Competition, 2nd Prize winner
Materials: Colorcore™ surfacing material by Formica Corporation

Product: Classical Cabinet
Designer: Paul Chiasson, New York, New York
Design Firm: P.D.C.C. Studio, New York, New York
Designed for: Colorcore™ "Surface & Ornament" Competition I and Exhibition
Awards: "Surface & Ornament" Competition, 4th Prize Winner
Materials: Colorcore™ surfacing material by Formica Corporation

Product: Tête-à-Tête
Designer: Stanley Tigerman, Chicago, Illinois
Design Firm: Tigerman, Fugman, McCurry
Chicago Illinois
Designed for: Colorcore ™ "Surface & Ornament"
Competition I and Exhibition
Materials: Colorcore ™ surfacing material by
Formica Corporation

Product: L System
Designer: Emilio Ambasz and Giancarlo Piretti
New York, New York
Designed for: Colorcore ™ "Surface & Ornament"
Competition I and Exhibition
Materials: Colorcore ™ surfacing material by
Formica Corporation

Product: Modern Post-Neo Table
Designer: Milton Glaser, New York New York
Design Firm: Milton Glaser Associates, New York, New
York
Designed for: Colorcore ™ "Surface & Ornament"
Competition I and Exhibition
Materials: Colorcore ™ surfacing material by
Formica Corporation

Product: Broken Length
Designer: Lella and Massimo Vignelli, New York,
              New York
Design Firm: Vignelli Associates, New York, New York
Designed for: Colorcore ™ "Surface & Ornament"
              Competition I and Exhibition
Materials: Colorcore ™ surfacing material by
              Formica Corporation

Product: Cart-Mobile
Designer: Ward Bennett, New York, New York
Designed for: Colorcore ™ "Surface & Ornament"
              Competition I and Exhibition
Materials: Colorcore ™ surfacing material by
              Formica Corporation

Product: Michael Graves Seating Collection
Designer: Michael Graves, Princeton, New Jersey
Client: Sunar/Hauserman, Norwalk, Connecticut
Materials: Bird's-eye maple with upholstery

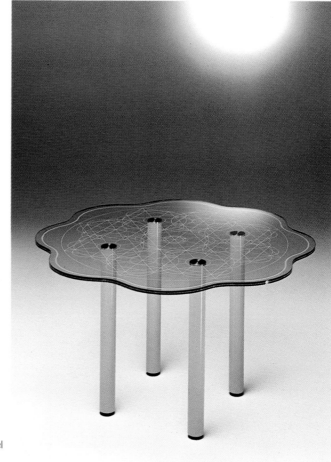

Product: Cinquecento
Designer: Alik Cavaliere
Client: Zanotta SPA, Milan, Italy
Materials: Surface: glass; Legs: burnished steel

Product: Imperiale
Designer: Achille Castiglioni
Client: Zanotta SPA, Milan, Italy
Materials: Frame: stainless steel; Armrests: wood;
Seat: cotton fabric; upholstered headrest

Product: Cabaret
Designer: Stefano Casciani
Client: Zanotta SPA, Milan, Italy
Materials: Steel; polyurethane foam

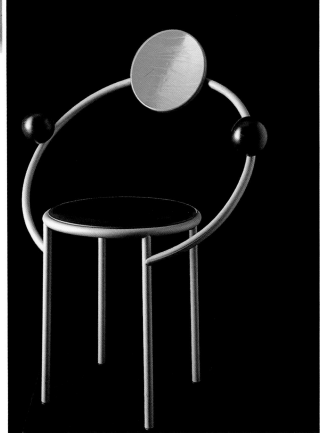

Product: First
Designer: Michele de Lucchi, Milan, Italy
Client: Memphis, Milan, Italy
Materials: Metal and wood

Product: Royal
Designer: Nathalie du Pasquier, Paris, France
Client: Memphis, Milan, Italy
Materials: Plastic laminate and printed cotton

Product: Experiment Collection
Designer: Yrjo Kukkapuro, Helsinki, Finland
Client: Avarte Oy, Helsinki, Finland
Materials: Seat and back: press-formed birch veneer, plastic laminate; Armrests: press-formed birch plywood; Legs: chrome-plated steel tube

Product: Sindbad
Designer: Vico Magistretti
Client: Cassina, Milan, Italy
Importer/
Distributor: Atelier International, Ltd., New York, New York
Materials: Base: black lacquered beechwood; Frame: welded steel; Body: molded polyurethane foam and Dacron

Product: Painted wood garden seat
Designer: Antti Nurmesniemi, Helsinki, Finland
Design Firm: Studio Nurmesniemi, Helsinki, Finland
Client: Vuokko Oy, Helsinki, Finland
Materials: Red beech, painted white, brass fixtures

Product: Steel wire garden seat
Designer: Antti Nurmesniemi, Helsinki, Finland
Design Firm: Studio Nurmesniemi, Helsinki, Finland
Client: Vuokko Oy, Helsinki, Finland
Materials: Epoxy-coated steel wire

Product: Trapezoid
Designer: James Evanson, New York, New York
Materials: Plastic laminate with lacquer

Product: Richard Meier Collection
Designer: Richard Meier, New York, New York
Client: Knoll International, New York, New York
Materials: Maple with black, white, or natural hand-
             rubbed finish

Product: The Capsule hotel bed
Designer: Kisho Kurokawa, Tokyo, Japan
Design Firm: Kisho Kurokawa Architect & Associates,
              Tokyo, Japan
Client: Kotobuki Seating Co. Ltd., Tokyo, Japan
Materials: Phenol resin modules molded in two
              halves and bolted together and stacked
              on steel frames

CESHOUSEWARESTOOLSAPPLIANCESHOUSEWARESTOOLSAPPLIANCESHOUSEWAR TOOLSAPPLIANCESHOUSEWAREST
CESHOUSEWARESTOOLSAPPLIANCESHOUSEWARESTOOLSAPPLIANCESHOUSEWAR

CTRONICSENTERTAINMENTHOMEELECTRONICSENTERTAINMENTHOMEELECTRON
AINMENTHOMEELECTRONICSENTERTAINMENTHOMEELECTRONICSENTERTAINMEN

GLIGHTINGLIGHTINGLIGHTINGLIGHTINGLIGHTINGLIGHTINGLIGHTINGLIGHTINGLIGHTINGLIGHTING
GLIGHTINGLIGHTINGLIGHTINGLIGHTINGLIGHTINGLIGHTINGLIGHTING TINGLIGHTINGLIGHTIN

TRESIDENTIALFURNISHINGSCONTRACTRESIDENTIALFURNISHINGSCONT
TIALFURNISHINGSCONTRACTRESIDENTIALFURNISHINGSCONTRACTRESI

SEQUIPMENTBUSINESSEQUIPMENTBUSINESSEQUIPMENTBUSINESSEQUIPMENTBUSINESSEQUIPMENTBUSINESSEQU
SEQUIPMENTBUSINESSEQUIPMENTBUSINESSEQUIPMENTBUSINESSEQUIPMENTBUSINESSEQUIPMENTBUSINESSEQU

EQUIPMENTMEDICALEQUIPMENTMEDICALEQUIPMENTMEDICALEQUIPMENTMEDICALEQUIPMENTMEDICALEQUIPMENT
NTMEDICALEQUIPMENTMEDICALEQUIPMENTMEDICALEQUIPMENTMEDICALEQUIPMENTMEDICALEQUIPMENTMEDICAL

RIALEQUIPMENTTRANSPORTATIONINDUSTRIALEQUIPMENTTRANSPORTATIONINDUSTRIALEQUIPMENTTRANSPORTAT
RIALEQUIPMENTTRANSPORTATIONINDUSTRIALEQUIPMENTTRANSPORTATIONINDUSTRIALEQUIPMENTTRANSPORTAT

IONALSPORTSEQUIPMENTRECREATIONALSPORTSEQUIPMENTRECREATIONALSPORTSEQUIPMENTRECREATIONALSPO
NTRECREATIONALSPORTSEQUIPMENTRECREATIONALSPORTSEQUIPMENTRECREATIONALSPORTSEQUIPMENTRECREA

STEXTILESTEXTILESTEXTILESTEXTILESTEXTILESTEXTILESTEXTILESTEXTILESTEXTILESTEXTILESTEXTILES
STEXTILESTEXTILESTEXTILESTEXTILESTEXTILESTEXTILESTEXTILESTEXTILESTEXTILESTEXTILESTEXTILES

FORTHEHANDICAPPEDDESIGNSFORTHEHANDICAPPEDDESIGNSFORTHEHANDICAPPEDDESIGNSFORTHEHANDICAPPED
HANDICAPPEDDESIGNSFORTHEHANDICAPPEDDESIGNSFORTHEHANDICAPPEDDESIGNSFORTHEHANDICAPPEDDESIGNS

Business Equipment

Perhaps no category more than that of business equipment exemplifies how the design industry has benefited from the recent and sudden growth of communications technology. As tele-communications have made the world a smaller place, it is designers who have helped to make this transition a comfortable one. As the complexities and capabilities of business equipment increase, so too, in direct proportion, must their simplicity and ease of function. More and more, it is a case of simplicity undercutting complexity.

Ease of operation is vital not only because of the growing capabilities of much of this equipment, but also because of the varied levels of electronic literacy of its users. Witness, for example, the Edge videotape editing console designed by Steinhilber & Deutsch, Associates. Part of the console's success is due to that fact that it is easily operated by users with any level of experience. Because its design helps to make its operation self-evident, the inexperienced user is able to concentrate on editing, rather than on the mastery of the controls.

Aside from this rather obvious point of ease of use, another apparent feature of contemporary business equipment is its compactness. Designer input is integral both to equipment which combines different communications functions and equipment which has simply become smaller, or even miniaturized. The growth in the variety of products which can be accommodated by the briefcase is matched in number only by the challenges they present to the designer.

A second, and no less important feature is compatibility. Whether it is the business itself that is expanding, or the business's need and use of electronics, or both, component systems which are designed to be updated to accommodate new equipment have a clear edge. And, as electronic literacy is on the rise, users demand new capabilities. Systems which can respond to this sophistication are meeting a real market demand. Compactness and compatibility—often approached simultaneously—are surely the two keynotes in the design of contemporary business equipment, and computer design is, of course, the most active arena for their development.

The MAD-1 microcomputer (the acronym is for Modular Advanced Design) designed by Mike Nuttall is a case in point. The unit is among the first small computers to use the powerful 80186 microprocessor—which has twice as many transistors in its quarter-inch silicon chip as its predecessor, the 8088. The 80186 integrates the fifteen to twenty chips previously required into a single integrated circuitry, in effect installing a full circuit board into a miniature case. But as significant is the fact that the 80186 can be used with the same instructions as the 8088. So, users of the MAD-1 can use most of the same software, in particular the business applications software designed for the IBM PC, but twice as fast. In addition, the compact MAD-1 is ergonomically designed: The slope of the low profile keyboard is reduced, the display monitor tilts and swivels to reduce eye and neck fatigue, a palm rest area supports the hands, and the modularity of the systems permits different configurations on the desk top.

The designers at I D Two of Grid's Compass portable computer faced even more extreme challenges. As the firm's director, Bill Moggridege, explains, "New technologies made a truly portable computer possible. Flat panel displays, bubble memory, low-profile keyboards, large-scale integration of logic, and small modems for the transmission of both voice and data via telephone lines all made it possible to develop for the first time a powerful machine which could fit into a briefcase." A team comprising both systems engineers and industrial designers developed a unit that weighed 9½ lbs. (4.3 kg.) and measured 11½" × 15½" × 2" (2 × 39 × 5 cm.). Its computing capabilities, meanwhile, were powerful enough to handle budgetary planning and, through the telephone line, could also retrieve programs, access centrally stored data, and send and receive messages by electronic mail. The housing for the entire unit was magnesium, a deviation from the standard plastic housing of portable computers, that was selected for its light weight and adaptability to precision tooling—which permitted additional design flexibility.

What distinguishes the Compass as much as its unconventional housing, advanced computing power in a portable size, and refined styling is the manner in which it was developed. Participating in its development were an industrial designer, a mechanical engineer, an electronics systems engineer, a logic and wiring engineer, and a staff member conversant with manufacturing processes. Because the unit does indeed "push packaging technology," the engineers recognized the need for industrial and mechanical design staff to collaborate with electronics logic experts. That industrial designers should work so closely with engineers in the start-up phase of product development—to determine performance as well as appearance—is indeed unique.

While larger business equipment manufacturers, such as IBM, have traditionally been conspicuous for the high-quality design of their products, smaller firms have rarely followed suit. The electronics industry—marked by the recent and rapid emergence of small firms—however, has been turning all this around by noting the fact that competitive design work in product development may be what determines the leading edge on the market. In judging the many innovations occurring in California's Silicon Valley, this re-evaluation of the designer/engineer relationship is not the least insignificant.

Clearly, the domain of the industrial business equipment designer has grown in recent years. Color, texture, material, and system image are no longer the only areas that answer to his specifications. His considerations have grown to include size, ergonomic adjustability, modularity within the system, and compatibility to other systems, to name a few. And as design in this category becomes more an issue of product development than of styling, it also becomes a research-based process. But on the other end, these same designers are becoming involved with marketing their products. Because the design strategy begins at an earlier stage, it is not surprising that it should be continued into a later one as well. That is, as the design strategy becomes more integral to the overall business strategy of a product, it has as much a place in marketing as it does in product development. Out of necessity, designers working in this field of equipment have become literate in new areas, recognizing the fact that sales may come to depend upon their recognition of design as an interdisciplinary medium. What all of this suggests is not simply that the context of the design profession has grown here, but that its lead may well be followed elsewhere.

Product: PCS-Cadmus 2200 terminal
Designer: Alexander Neumeister
               Munich, West Germany
Design Firm: Neumeister Design
               Munich, West Germany
Client: Periphere Computer Systeme GmbH
               Munich, West Germany
Materials: Anti-glare display unit; low contrast
               casing; tilting mechanism; laser beam
               printer

Product: Mad-1 computer
Designer: Mike Nuttall
               Palo Alto, California
Design Firms: ID Two
               and Dave Kelley Design
               Palo Alto, California
Client: Mad Computer Inc.
               Santa Clara, California
Materials: ABS housing
Photo Credit: Jack Christianson

Product: Pronto Series 16 computer
Design Firm: Ron Loosen Associates
               Los Alamitos, California
Client: Pronto Computers
               Torrence, California
Awards: 1983 *Industrial Design* magazine
               Design Review selection
Materials: Sheet metal with foam front electronics
               box; entire unit is painted in polane

Product:	WY-1000 terminal
Designer:	Jim Sacherman
	Palo Alto, California
Design Firm:	Matrix Product Design, Inc.
	Palo Alto, California
Client:	Wyse Technology
	San Jose, California
Materials:	Low-profile sculptures keyboard
Photo credit:	Henrik Kam

Product:	ITT 3840 computer work station and disc module
Design Firm:	Fischer-Design
	Scottsdale, Arizona
Client:	Standard Elektrik Lorenz, subsidiary of ITT
	Munich, West Germany
Materials:	Fire-retardant Noryl structural foam

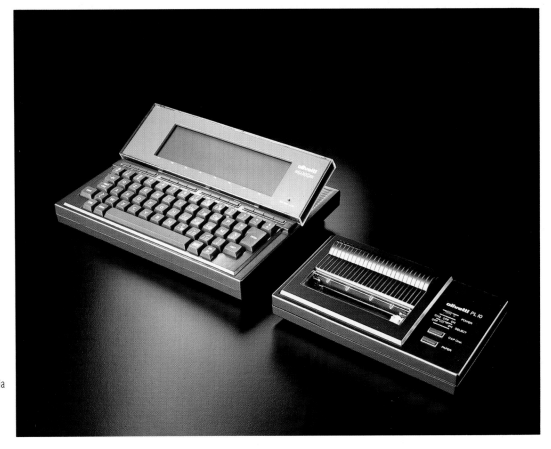

Product:	M 10 portable computer
Designers:	Perry A. King and Antonio Macchi Cassia
	Milan, Italy
Client:	Ing. C. Olivetti & C. S.p.A.
	Ivrea, Italy
Awards:	1983 SMAU Design Award

Product: Wang Professional Computer
Designers: Karen L. Usab, Lawrence M. Kuba,
Douglas C. Dayton,
and Paul W. Porter
Lowell, Massachusetts
Client: Wang Laboratories Inc.
Lowell, Massachusetts
Materials: Sheet metal CPU housing; structural
foam molded monitor base; cast
aluminum monitor arm; extruded
aluminum desk clamp; monitor and
keyboard housing and CPU front bezel:
injection-molded

Product: WorkSlate
Designer: Mike Nuttall
Palo Alto, California
Design Firm: Matrix Product Design Inc.
Palo Alto, California
Client: Convergent Technologies, Inc.
Santa Clara, California
Materials: Injection-molded ABS
Photo Credit: Light Language, San Francisco

Product: Iskrascope LCD—digital osciloscope,
digital multimeter, data processor, and
transient recorder
Designer: Ljuban Klojcnik
Kranj, Yugoslavia
Design Firm: Iskra Kibernetika
Kranj, Yugoslavia
Client: Iskra Commerce
Ljubljana, Yugoslavia
Materials: ABS plastic

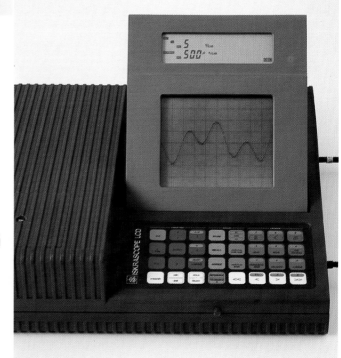

Product: Micronunciator alarm annunciator
Designers: D. Celine, M. Gans, L. Thole, and design
team,
Control Logic (Pty) Ltd.
Client: Control Logic (Pty) Ltd.
Durban, South Africa
Awards: 1982 Shell Design Award

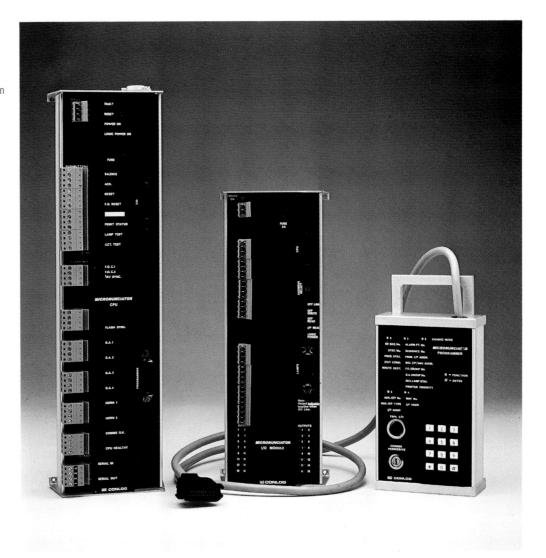

Product: Omeg/Balco digital insulation and
continuity tester
(This unit is used for installation and
maintainence of domestic
and industrial wiring layouts)
Designer: K. W. Junker and H. M. Teubner
Client: Omnitec Institute and Electronic
Manufacturers (Pty) Ltd.
Excom, South Africa
Awards: 1982 Shell Design Award
Materials: Polycarbonate casing

Product: Y-688³² total error corrector video
processor
Designer: Bruce Pharr, design staff
Fortel Inc.
Design Firm: Penney & Bernstein
New York, New York
Client: Fortel Inc.
Atlanta, Georgia
Materials: Aluminum housing

Product: Disa Telephone 1200 Type Range
Designers: K. Hartiani, R. Derbyshire and design
team,
Telephone Manufacturers of South Africa;
J. A. Raath and B. A. Bets, and design
team,
Department of Posts and
Telecommunications;
Roger Williams Associates
Pretoria, South Africa
Client: Telephone Manufacturers of South Africa
Springs, South Africa
Awards: 1982 Shell Design Award

Product: Handheld laser
Designer: William Sklaroff
Design Firm: William Sklaroff Design Associates
Philadelphia, Pennsylvania
Client: Metrologic Instruments Inc.
Bellmaur, New Jersey
Materials: ABS Cycolac housing

Product: Record 2 video detail booster
Designer: Bruce Pharr, design staff
Fortel Inc.
Design Firm: Penney & Bernstein
New York, New York
Client: Fortel Inc.
Atlanta, Georgia
Materials: Aluminum housing

Product: Cafe-Bar Services
Client: Burns, Philp & Company Limited
Sydney, Australia

CHAPTER **6**

Medical Equipment

Until recently, aesthetic design development of medical equipment has lagged far behind the sophisticated "state-of-the-art" technology which the equipment houses. Although this is no longer always the case, the delayed aesthetic development suggests that the design of medical equipment is an area in which the state of change continues to invite innovation.

What most signals the raised design consciousness of contemporary medical equipment is the attention paid to human factors engineering. While the role of human factors in design has certainly grown over the past ten years, nowhere is it so vital, or in such demand, as in the medical environment. It is, of course, crucial that an office chair comfortably support the human frame. Yet the comfort provided by a CT scanner detecting the brain tissues of an accident victim, and the convenience with which it can be operated by the technician and monitored by the radiologist in an emergency situation are surely on a different level. Ergonomics has a different meaning altogether in the life-and-death situations of a hospital.

What distinguishes medical equipment even more is the range of users it must address—the doctors and technicians who operate the equipment; the patients; and often, the service personnel. That medical products from dental equipment to nuclear magnetic resonance scanning systems are being designed to consider the entire range of users indeed sets them apart from their predecessors.

One product that first addressed these multivaried needs was the CT (computerized tomography) scanner, which captures a cross-sectional image of the human anatomy with X-rays, and then reconstructs the image electronically. With the development of its technology in the mid-1970s came the recognition that human factors would be integral to its application. The GE 9800 unit responds in a number of ways: The aperture of the gantry—the housing unit for the tube and detector—is larger than that of early models, and is thus less intimidating to the patient; softened edges of the gantry and the table both lessen the perceived volume and make for a more "human" appearance. The equipment rests on a small dark base. This gives it the illusion of floating, making it appear lighter and further diminishing its potentially threatening appearance. Finally, the scanner computers are located in a separate room—in part because their humming noise can disturb patients. As the designer for the scanner stated, it was the industrial design analysis "of user needs and CAD patient positioning study that established the scan geometry and patient positioning parameters permitting maximum tunnel opening, gantry tilt, and patient travel for improved patient access and scannability."

The participation of industrial designers in the development of NMR (nuclear magnetic resonance) scanners is even greater, as the unit makes heavier human factors demands. NMR collects chemical information of atoms by using the magnetic qualities of their nuclei. The NMR units, however, must generate a magnetic field thousands of times greater than the earth's, and as a result, some weigh over five tons. The problems confronting designers are: maintaining a uniform magnetic field by keeping the housing of the equipment, surrounding equipment, patients, and personnel free of ferrous materials; providing doctors and technicians with easy access to patients; and diminishing patient apprehension at being confined in a tube not much larger than his or her own body. Most manufacturers of these systems will agree that the human factors input of industrial designers and their collaboration with engineers has been crucial in resolving patient orientation, the placement of display equipment, means of patient/operator contact, and metal detection for the surrounding area and personnel.

While CT and NMR systems must consider human factors on a rather expansive scale, the manner in which smaller pieces of equipment meets these demands is no less significant. The Corning 102 Printer is a case in point. Designed to be used with existing blood analysis instrumentation, the printer meets the lab's needs for a permanent, sequential record of daily test and calibration results. It was the industrial designer's input which suggested that controls traditionally located internally and factory preset be made "user accessible" on the rear of the unit. The result was also a "user-installable" printer, which eliminated the need for a field service engineer. Likewise, the Corning designers approached the design of the Digital pH meter "from the inside out, dealing with the operational and perceptual issues before the structural ones." The comprehensive approach resulted in a design that, through a series of questions and statements, guides the user—who in all likelihood has had little or no previous exposure to the instrument—though the measurement sequence. The designers also specified that because a large LCD would "perform poorly in the extreme temperatures, vibrations, and shocks of industrial environments," the display medium be divided into two components—a standard seven-segment LED for numeric information, and a sixteen-segment alphanumeric LED for the parameters and instructions. A sealed touch panel, also geared to withstand the rigors of the industrial environment, reduced the number of key positions from 27 to 19, "simplifying operation and improving flexibility." A five-language capability for all display information was incorporated into the system to accommodate a world market. What all this points out most clearly is that the inside-out approach to design—by involving designers with systems engineers—results in a product whose

fine-tuned aesthetics, coherent product image, ease of operation, and human factors recognition all correspond to the producer's high level of technology.

Finally, in discussing the user convenience of medical equipment, an irony becomes apparent: While the equipment must appear accessible and friendly, it should not necessarily appear *too* friendly or *too* accessible. The medical procedures carried out by this equipment are presumably of a serious nature, and to undermine this would also be to undermine the confidence of the patient. The equipment must be absolutely unintimidating, but it must also simultaneously convey a certain seriousness that will emphasize its capability and competence, thus reassuring the patient. While paradox may seem to prevail here, designers whose products can assimilate and balance contradictions are perhaps best recognizing the complex frame of mind of their users, and the complex situations of their use.

That the technology supporting most of these products is so recent, and in such a state of evolution, works both for and against the design of the equipment. Evolving products run the risk of being outdated even by the time they are introduced on the market; on the other hand, the opportunity exists to establish standards in an area of design that remains relatively uncharted. Designers who acknowledge the dual aspects of this situation will recognize the precarious position held by the design of their products. By acting on it, they will be contributing to the area of design that perhaps most pleads for fine tuning.

Product: Digital pH meter
Designers: Scott Mathis and Robert Potts
Industrial Design Dept., Corning Medical
Medfield, Massachusetts
Client: Corning Science Products
Medfield, Massachusetts
Awards: 1983 IDSA Industrial Design Excellence
Award
Materials: Molded Noryl foam; textured
polyurethane finish; power supply
chassis: pressure die-cast in aluminum;
embossed touchpanel and display:
fabricated of PVC; electrode arm and
base: injection-molded modified
polypropylene

Product: Model 102 printer
Designer: John F. Buchholz, Corning Medical
Medfield, Massachusetts
Client: Corning Medical
Medfield, Massachusetts
Awards: 1983 IDSA Industrial Design Excellence
Award
Materials: Noryl structural foam front housing with
sonically welded boss inserts; back
panel: thermoformed flame retardent
ABS; silkscreened polycarbonate label
provides interchangeable graphics on
rear panel

Product: Driv-Lok Grooved Pin in aortic punch
Designer: Staff design, Driv-Lok, Inc.
Sycamore, Illinois
Client: Driv-Lok, Inc.
Sycamore, Illinois
Materials: Stainless steel

Product: Hypo-Count II blood glucose monitor
Designers: Staff design, Hypoguard Ltd. and Bernard
            Sams
            Suffolk, England
Client: Hypoguard Ltd.
            Suffolk, England
Awards: 1983 Design Council Award

Product: Hematrak™, Geometric Data Corporation
Designer: William Sklaroff
Design Firm: William Sklaroff Design Associates
             Philadelphia, Pennsylvania
Client: Geometric Data Corporation
             division of SmithKlein Beckman
             Wayne, Pennsylvania
Materials: Extruded aluminum; ABS plastic housing

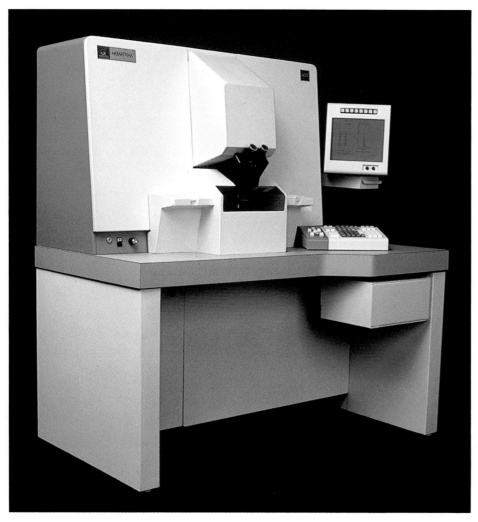

Product: Electrophoresis densitometer
Designers: Gianfranco Zaccai, Instrumentation
            Laboratory Inc.
            Lexington, Massachusetts
Client: Instrumentation Laboratory Inc.
            Lexington, Massachusetts
Materials: Housing: Noryl structural foam;
            polyurethane painted finish

Product: Electronic Thermometer with LCD
Readout
Designers: Engineering staff, Matsushita Electrical
and
Industrial Company of Japan
Osaka, Japan
Client: Panasonic Company
Division of Matsushita Electric
Corporation of America
Secaucus, New Jersey
Materials: ABS plastic

Product: PO₂rtable Oxygen Monitor
Designers: Staff design, Instrumentation Laboratory
Lexington, Massachusetts
Client: Instrumentation Laboratory, Inc.
Lexington, Massachusetts
Awards: Industrial Design magazine
1983 Design Review selection
Materials: Exterior: injection-molded in flame
retardant cycolac ABS; kickstand:
stainless steel

Product: 943 Flame Photometer
Designer: Gianfranco Zaccai
Boston, Massachusetts
Client: Instrumentation Laboratory SpA
Milan, Italy
Awards: 1982 *Industrial Design* magazine
Design Review selection
1983 IDSA Industrial Design Excellence
Award
Materials: Housing: sheet aluminum and structural
foam with polyurethane finish; membrane
keyboard/display control panel:
polycarbonate

Product: Pillow Speaker
(patient communications signalling
device)
Designer: William Sklaroff
Design firm: William Sklaroff Design Associates
Philadelphia, Pennsylvania
Client: Executone Inc.
Jericho, New York
Materials: ABS "cycolac" housing

Product: Pherotron modular densitometer system
Design Firm: Neumeister Design
Munich, West Germany
Client: LRE Medizintechnik
Munich, West Germany

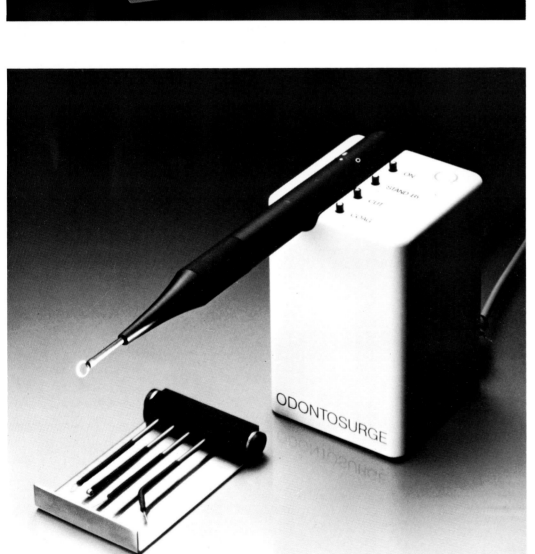

Product: Odontosurge
Designer: David Lewis and Lennart Goof
Hørsholm, Denmark
Client: A/S L. Goof
Hørsholm, Denmark
Awards: 1982 Danish Design Council Award

Industrial Equipment and Transportation

What most distinguishes the design of transportation and heavy industry from other categories of design are the stringent demands made upon it by the environment. In most areas of design, the designer must contend with the product and the user alone. Here, however, he must also consider how the product addresses the environment. This is all the more relevant at a time in history when conservation has become a particularly sensitive, if not critical, issue.

Consider, for example, the Roulund floating oil boom, designed to stop the spread of oil slicks caused by leaks in drilling rigs and ships. The product is simply conceived and simply executed; modular rubber floats are large enough to prevent spillage, and have been designed to lie on the water's surface at an angle which will stabilize them when they are towed in a U-shape—enough to withstand collisions with ships. They are also easily cleaned and easily transported in containers, either by plane or truck to the accident site. Reflector strips identify inside and out. Both in concept and design, the product meets urgent contemporary demands of the environment in a straightforward and effective manner.

Magnetic levitation trains, such as the Transrapid 06 designed by Alexander Neumeister, show the same attention, though on a far grander scale. The train, designed along the principles of electromagnetic levitation, run along their tracks without any frictional contact. In essence, ferromagnetic armature rails of the track and electromagnets fitted to the train maneuver transit; levitation magnets pull the train up to the track while guidance magnets keep it centered. The elevated tracks demand minimal space and disruption of the countryside; the noise level and energy consumption are low and the electric drive system does not emit gases or fumes. Clearly, this is an example of a rapid transit system well-tuned to its environment. Whether it is a simply constructed oil boom or the new technology for rapid transit, there is a direct equation between the sophistication of the products in this category and their recognition of the affect they may have on an often fragile environment.

The aerodynamic styling of the Transrapid 06 is also evident elsewhere in transportation design. More emphatic streamlining for diminished air resistance and susceptibility to crosswinds are as apparent in automobile design. As Toyota states about its 1984 van, "The vehicle spent a lot of time in the wind tunnel during its early design stages." What resulted was an aerodynamically styled front end with a 40 degree rake to the windshield, and body lines that yield a low drag coefficient of .40 (which is lower than even some passenger cars). The sloping front and roofline also make for a downforce that increases stability at high speeds. Likewise, wind tunnel research contributed to the design of the 1984 Chevrolet Corvette. The airflow through its passenger compartment and engine was as thoughtfully considered as the airflow over the outside of the car. As the designer explains, "Air is admitted from under the front end rather than through the traditional grille; both drag and lift are minimized, as is wind, noise, and dirt contamination." The overall drag coefficient in this case is .341.

The Corvette's ergonomic interior is as unique as its aerodynamic exterior, another aspect appearing more frequently in contemporary automobile design. Ergonomically designed car seats consider two things—a form which gives the human frame maximum support, and a high degree of adjustability for individual contours.

Although these features may not come as a surprise in the Corvette—which its designers refer to as "a driver's car rather than a passenger car . . . that must combine excellent roadholding with immediate response and a high degree of personal interaction for the driver . . ." —their appearance in more standard vehicles suggests that another mark of contemporary design is that ergonomics in the automobile is no longer limited to luxury cars.

Human factors are also making a strong showing in the control display designs of transportation vehicles. As the designers of the Corvette explain, "The controls are designed for easy reach, and liquid crystal digital displays deliver instant readings of engine condition and driving range." While automobiles are perhaps the most obvious arena for human factored controls, they are evident elsewhere as well. The Crown Series TS Turret Sideloader designed by Richardson/Smith is a case in point. The designers' research determined not only the placement of controls, but in some cases, generated the graphics as well. The panel for the sideloader includes controls for rotation, traverse, forward and reverse travel, a discharge indicator, emergency override switches, a horn button, and a lighted function display panel. The designers discovered through their research that a combination of established and new codes would most effectively indicate the full range of these functions. This, too, sets apart contemporary vehicles and transport equipment—the clear placement and graphics of controls which recognize human factors specifications. As products are designed more and more for international markets, this attention to graphics, and to universal signage in particular, will increase all the more.

Finally, in this category of design, the use of new materials cannot be overlooked. The Avtek 400, for example, a six- to nine-passenger twin turboprop plane, uses lightweight, high-strength composites of Kevlar aramid fiber and honeycomb of Nomex aramid fiber; the weight of the plane is 3,100 lbs. (1,406 kg.), roughly half that of similar aircraft. Kevlar—stronger than steel and aluminum but lighter than fiberglass—has rather obvious applications in aircraft construction. With a top speed of 425 miles (684 km.) per hour and the ability to reach an altitude of 10,000 feet (3048 m.) in one minute and fifty seconds, the plane's performance surpasses that of comparably sized aircraft. Again, it is the design process—here the application of new materials—which has revolutionized the product by so dramatically upgrading its performance.

The design of contemporary transportation and heavy industry then, is signalled by a number of features; most important, it tends to acknowledge the environment which is to accommodate it. Add to this more dramatic aerodynamic styling, ergonomic finetuning, and the application of new materials, and it becomes evident that the transitions occurring here render a new vitality for the design of this equipment.

Product: 1984 Chevrolet Corvette
Designers: General Motors Design, Warren,
             Michigan
Client: Chevrolet Motor Division
             General Motors Corporation
             Warren, Michigan
Awards: 1983 IDSA Industrial Design Excellence
             Award
Materials: Body: fiberglass formed on matched dies
             with panels designed for easy repair;
             bumpers: elastomeric with protective
             molding along the body side; micro-
             electric computer system; four-wheel
             independent suspension with forged
             aluminum guide arms and glass fiber leaf
             springs tuned to specially designed tires

Product: LRC Train interior
Designer: Morley Smith
               Montreal, Quebec, Canada
Design Firm: GSM Design Inc.
               Montreal, Quebec, Canada
Client: VIA Rail Canada
               Montreal, Quebec, Canada
Materials: Seats: fiberglass-reinforced polyester;
               cushions: neoprene foam; upholstery:
               wool and nylon; floorcovering: nylon;
               baggage compartments: vacuum-formed
               ABS plastic; interior panels: melamine
               laminate

Product: GSM Taxi
Designer: Morley Smith
              Montreal, Quebec, Canada
Design Firm: GSM Design Inc.
              Montreal, Quebec, Canada
Awards: Design Canada Special Award 1982 for
              research and innovation
Materials: Steel main frame; tubular subframe;
              energy-absorbing perimetric bumper;
              lower body section: fiberglass moldings
              bolted to subframe; bumper and side
              panel system: urethane; interior lining:
              rigid plastic door and roof panels and
              window surrounds; taxi can
              accommodate wheelchair passenger

Product: Gas-Trac combustible gas detector
Design Firm: Dale E. Fahnstrom Design
               Riverside, Illinois
Client: Epsilon Lambda Electronics
               Batavia, Illinois
Awards: 1981 *Industrial Design* magazine
               Design Review special mention
Materials: Component cover, probe cover, and
               switch injection-molded ABS; probe clip
               and thumbwheel: black nylon; lanyard
               loop: stainless steel; battery chips:
               phosphor bronze; escutcheon plate:
               aluminum; gooseneck: flexible chrome-
               plated steel

Product: Transrapid 06 magnetic levitation train
Designer: Alexander Neumeister
               Munich, West Germany
Design Firm: Neumeister Design
               Munich, West Germany

Product:	AVTEK 400
Designers:	William Taylor, Palm Desert, California
	Al Mooney, Ingram, Texas
Client:	Avtek Corporation
	Camarillo, California
Materials:	Airframe: honeycomb of "Nomex"
	aramid fiber sandwiched between skins
	of "Kevlar" aramid fiber

Product: Boeing 767 interior
Design Firm: Walter Dorwin Teague Associates
              New York, New York
              in collaboration with Boeing Engineers
              Boeing Commercial Airplane Company
              Seattle, Washington
Client: Boeing Commercial Airplane Company
              Seattle, Washington
Materials: Compartments and interior hard
              surfaces: formed Nomex™ fire-retardant,
              crushed-core honeycomb materials;
              opaque Tedlar™ pre-printed or plain
              material silkscreened to specialized
              airline design; clear Tedlar protective
              film; fabrics: wool or wool blends
              manufactured to specifications of each
              airline

Product: Westland 30 Series helicopter
Designers: R. A. Doe, G. H. Humphrey, D.E.H. Balmford
R. E. Swinfield, F. G. Rivers, P. Brammer, and B. Main
Client: Westland Helicopters Ltd.
Somerset, England
Awards: The Duke of Edinburgh's Designer's Prize
1983 Design Council Award
Materials: Twin Rolls-Royce Gem 60 engines; raft subframe system; elastomeric engine mountings; transmission health monitoring

Product: Kongskilde rotacrat
             (This unit is made to fit after the harrow
             behind a tractor; after the harrow pulls up
             the soil, the rotacraft crumbles it)
Designer: Finn Ulrich Jensen
Client: Kongskilde Maskinfabrik A/S
             Sorø, Denmark
Awards: 1982 Danish Design Council Award
Materials: Round spring bars for the rotarods;
             sectional discs stabilized by the counter-
             pressures of the rotarods; modular
             construction

Product: RO-BOOM, Roulund floating oil boom
(This product is used to trap and halt the
spread of oil slicks emitted by drilling
rigs and ships)
Designers: H. O. Holgersen and L. B. Rasmussen
Client: A/S Roulunds Fabriker
Odense, Denmark
Awards: 1982 Danish Design Council award
Materials: Rubber; modular construction for easy
transportation

Product: HUP-180 portable hydraulic pump
Designers: Joe Sonderman and Ed Montague
Design/Joe Sonderman, Inc., Charlotte,
North Carolina
Al Lefler, Fred Schultze, and Darril
Plummer
Duff-Norton Company, Charlotte, North
Carolina
Client: Duff-Norton Company
Charlotte, North Carolina
Materials: Cover piece: rotationally molded low-
intensity linear polyethylene with
inherent texture (in mold); reservoir
piece: sand-cast aluminum reservoir
dipped in Acid F bath to eliminate flash
removal abrasions and achieve matte
silver finish; black plastic valve control
knob; steel toggle power switch with
black rubber boot

Product: Airless I MK II line marking machine
Designer: Brian Glassel
Client: Dyco Products
            Melbourne, Australia
Materials: Steel chassis with fiberglass covers

Product: G. Series frontlift trucks
Designers: W. Wardle, B. Lowes, P. Ralph
Design Firm: Peter Ralph Design Associates
Client: LancerBoss Ltd.
                Bedfordshire, England
Awards: 1983 Design Council Award
Materials: Acoustically and thermally insulated cab;
                driving seat and control console rotate
                through 180 degrees

Product: Series TS Turret sideloader
Design Firm: Richardson/Smith
Worthington, Ohio
Client: Crown Controls Corporation
New Bremen, Ohio
Materials: Frame and mast: steel; access panels,
seat covers, instrument panels: vacuum-
formed ABS plastic

Product: Articulated 3-axle "Quick Drop" hopper
               (This system is used for loading,
               transporting, and discharging ores in
               underground mines)
Designer: P. Prins
               Brakpan, South Africa
Client: Austral Engineering Works (Pty)
               Brakpan, South Africa
Awards: 1982 Shell Design Award for Engineering
               Product
Materials: Two-module assembly, pivotally
               connected to allow the system to
               articulate; to control articulation, a third
               wheel set and assembly is placed
               between modules and is pivotally
               connected to them. The configuration
               permits more accurate steering and
               stability on sharp turns and uneven
               tracks.

Product: Towing tractor equipment for forestry
               work, prototype
Designer: Peter Tucny
               Prag/CSSR, West Germany
Awards: 1983 Braun Citation for Technical Design

Product: Explosion-proof forklift truck, prototype
Designer: Wolfgang Hesse and Erich Kruse
Braunschweig, West Germany
Awards:: 1983 Braun Prize for Technical Design

Product: Austpole rebutting machine
(This product is used to reclaim power
poles with groundline problems caused
by rot, accident, or fire)
Client: Austpole Pty. Ltd
Victoria, Australia

Recreational and Sports Equipment

The contemporary passion for physical fitness has spawned not only good health for its practitioners, but also a renewed attention to the gear and equipment with which it can be achieved. Not surprisingly, the exuberance that accompanies the physical activity appears to be matched by a rejuvenation in the design of sports gear.

Designers who recognize the growing marketability of sports products find that using new materials is one way to update old products. Note the Force Fin designed by Bob Evans. Made of polyurethane instead of rubber, it is much more flexible than the conventional fin—and without the conventional ribbing, it can move in any direction, without veering at awkward angles. Moreover, as the designer points out, "The Force Fin folds down on the upkick to reduce water resistance and snaps open for full power on the downstroke. Swimming with the Force Fin at first gives the impression that nothing has been attached to your foot at all, because the water flows backward rather than up and down. You don't have to work hard to make the flexible Force Fin work."

Likewise, the Nike cross country ski racing boot, designed by Trip Allen and Ken Geer, re-examines a traditional piece of equipment. Its redesign is due both to engineering *and* material. As the IDEA jury pointed out, the design addresses "two seemingly incompatible objectives—to simultaneously improve the skier's stability and turning control." The sole of the Nike boot has two parallel ridges running lengthwise along the outer bottom edges. Between these ridges is a cavity that accommodates the ski. By interlocking, the boot and ski become an "integrated turning control system." Moreover, the soles of the boots are unique in their use of Pebax, a specialty resin that has "a feel and performance similar to rubber." Pebax also fuses to itself in molding and eliminates manufacturing problems such as molding-in, or cementing rubber inserts.

The application of new materials, however, is not limited to traditional products. In some cases, such as the "Lance" speed skiing suit designed by Edward Roeanick, new materials are the inspiration for altogether new products. The designer used Dunlopreme 12 foam to form fairings attached to the backs of the arms and legs of the ski suit, and D7 foam in the hood section. A tail was molded in Dunloflex high resilience foam. The result was an aerodynamically shaped suit designed to reduce drag and increase speed, in a sport in which new records are set by milliseconds. Although the suit has not yet contributed to any new records, the idea this prototype promotes is that lightweight, aerodynamically styled foam may do more to enhance speed than the skintight attire favored by most speed skiers. Also implicit is the idea that, by way of new materials, design can suggest the future direction—or further refinement—of certain sports.

Witness as well the Pamir isothermic tunnel tent designed especially to endure—and to let its users endure—extremely cold temperatures. The tent is double-walled, with an outer wall of breatheable silver polyester blizzard that provides thermal insulation, and remains supple even in extremely low temperatures. The inner tent is 100 percent cotton. Two sheets of nylon make up the floor, and for maximum insulation a sheet of closed cellfoam can be inserted between them. In this case, clearly, it is the application of new materials that will permit campers to remain outdoors for longer times and in colder temperatures. Once again, it is through the use of material

that the sport allows the user to push his own endurance and skill to even greater limits.

The use of new materials alone does not distinguish contemporary sports gear; physical fitness is achieved these days in new ways and new places, and this, too, determines how the equipment is designed. While deep-sea divers and speed skiers tend to rely upon the local geography to practice their sports and use new high-tech gear, urban dwellers must often make do with the less awesome terrain of an apartment or studio to maintain their physical prowess. The recent array of home exercise tools and machines is evidence that this is indeed possible. Equipment for sports that are to be pursued within these confines, however, must meet a rather different set of demands. That is, these activities do not bring with them the stunning views, breathtaking speeds, or any of the other kinds of gratification offered by outdoor sports. The singular reward is physical fitness, and after a long and demanding day at the office, for example, this reward can pale for even the most disciplined and devoted athlete. So, then, this sports gear must invite and motivate the user, sometimes even suggesting (against all evidence to the contrary) that its operation is effortless. Hence the challenge to the designer. It is one well met by the Amerec 610 Precision Rowing Machine: Not only does the design make its operation self-evident, but the machine also looks comfortable.

Equipment designed for urban athletes must also consider space savings; that it be lightweight, portable, foldable, or otherwise collapsible poses to the designer another set of stringent demands. The foldable bicycle and prototype for a folding motorcycle shown here both offer efficient solutions. Although neither is currently being mass produced, both suggest that the convenience with which such items can be stored may well figure more in the future of their design and marketing.

Overall, the design of contemporary sports equipment appears to be continuing a tradition established in the last 20 years; in which the application of new materials and technologies to the traditional gear introduces untraditional efficiency, speed, strength, or effectiveness, thereby enhancing the skill and technique of the user. Thus, ski poles are bent for aerodynamics; baseball bats, tennis rackets, and skis are no longer necessarily made of wood but of plastics, fiberglass, aluminum, and combinations of unconventional materials. While these certainly add to the durability of the equipment, more to the point is that they add to what the athlete is actually able to achieve—in speed, in strength, or in power. Often, in the end, it is the design process—including the applications of new materials—that most changes the nature of the sport.

Product: Amerec 610 Precision Rowing Machine
Designer: David B. Smith, David Imanaka, and
                Burns D. Smith
                Redmond, Washington
Design Firm: Precor
                Redmond, Washington
Client: Amerec Corp.
                Bellevue, Washington
Awards: *Industrial Design* magazine
                1982 Design Review Selection
Materials: Frame and adjustable clamps: extruded
                aluminum; rowing arms: stainless steel;
                bushings, rowing arms, connectors,
                bumpers: injection-molded Delrin; foot
                pedals: structural foam; foot straps:
                velcro; seat: vinyl; elastic shock
                absorbers: neoprene; seat rollers:
                injection-molded nylon with capsulated
                ball bearings

Product: Force Fin
Designer: Bob Evans
              Santa Barbara, California
Client: BG Watersports
              Redondo Beach, California
Materials: Polyurethane; adjustable nylon straps

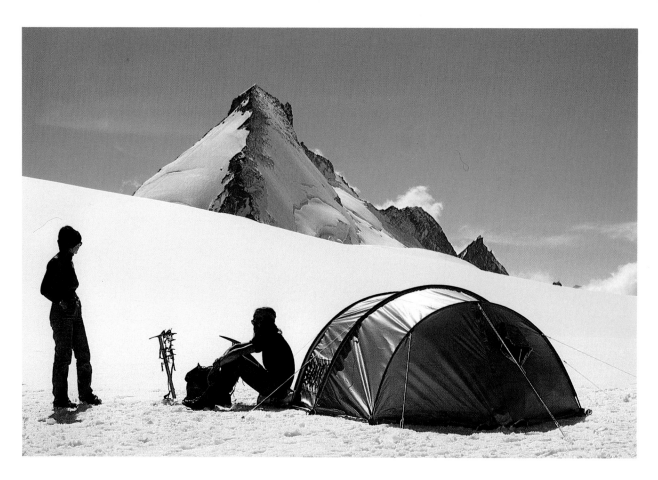

Product: Alpino Pamir III isothermic tunnel tent
Designer: Andre Heddebaut
Client: Alpino
Renaix, Belgium
Awards: 1983 Belgian Design Centre Signe d'Or
Materials: Inner tent: 100 percent lightweight cotton; outer tent: silver polyester; floor: two-sheet nylon; frame: lightweight aluminum alloy

Product: Eclipse Saddlepack
Designer: W. Shaun Jackson
Ann Arbor, Michigan
Design Firm: Eclipse Inc.
Ann Arbor, Michigan
Awards: 1982 IDSA Industrial Design Excellence Award
Materials: 1000 denier Cordura nylon; velcro fasteners; neoprene pad; plated steel hardware

Product: Lance ski suit
Designer: Edward Roeanick
Awards: 1983 Dunlopillo Design Award first prize
Materials: Fairings at the backs of arms and legs:
            Dunlopreme D12 foam; hood section at
            back of neck: D12 foam; molded
            Dunloflex high resilience foam; red,
            satin-finished tricot

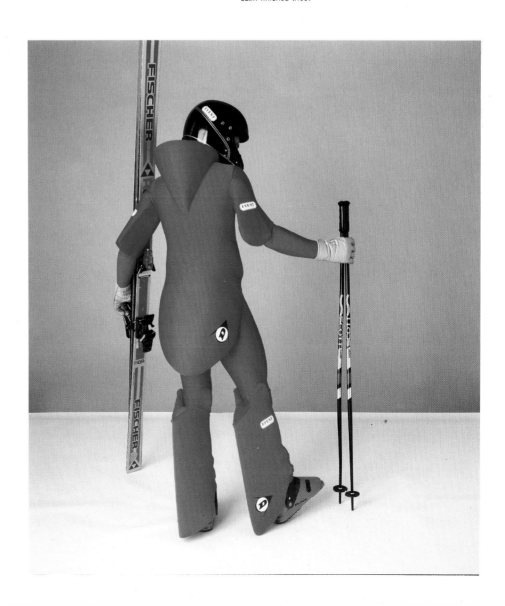

Textiles

Design of the late 1970s and early 1980s is indelibly marked by a renewed appreciation for color and ornament. Pattern, the decorated surface, and overall visual embellishment have all reappeared in architecture, furnishings, and even business equipment. But there is perhaps no area of design that has benefited more from this new spirit than fabrics and textiles. At long last, the extravagance of the 1960s and the cool colors and beiges of the 1970s have given way to a more exuberant, though controlled, palette.

It is this sense of control, perhaps, that most characterizes the contemporary excitement in color and pattern. As Jack Lenor Larsen and Mildred Constantine point out in their book *The Art Fabric: Mainstream*, "The pendulum has so strongly swung away from the highly charged, romantic expression of the sixties. The new classicism that has replaced it, is cerebral, disciplined, pure, and ordered." It is the antithesis of the more adventuresome, romantic, emotional, and often heroic spirit that preceded it.

Because this appetite for decoration has such a sense of symmetry and suggests a return to pattern, it is only logical that it should make itself so evident in textiles. For textiles—themselves based on the logic of the grid—by nature imply pattern, repetition, and continuity. The simple fact of its weave associates it with logic and order. Still, the sense of pattern and continuity in such evidence in contemporary textiles is not as rigid as it might be. Pattern has reappeared, but it is not as repetitive as one might expect. Subtle shifts in color, gradations in tone, and motifs that are repeated only irregularly are ways in which pattern is established, and then, just slightly, thrown off.

The new appreciation for color in fabrics is especially apparent in contract office applications. That is, upholstery and textiles for the office are now often part of a much larger coordinated color palette. Designer Clino Castelli suggests that it is not only a renewed interest in color, but also an entirely different way of perceiving color. "Color," he says, "is perhaps the single most noticeable imposition of the imposed space. Our reactions to color are emotional, visceral, extremely subjective." He also goes on to attribute this recent change in color preference to the influence of the electronic media. Castelli maintains that the colors of electronic transmission—such as those we see on television—are formed by numerous color overlays, an additive synthesis that is significantly different from "the subtractive colors of the print media." The result is what Castelli calls the "polychromatic tonal tendency," that is, the simultaneous presence of several less saturated colors. Even neutrals, he says, have distinguishable hues. Castelli's program of colors, fabrics, and finishes for the Herman Miller Action Office (shown in Chapter 4) is based on this theory of color. It is a coordination of several tones within one space—a polychromatic rather than a monochromatic environment.

Likewise, the Walker/Group has initiated a Coordinated Design Program with contract manufacturers in carpets, fabrics, laminates, and ceramic tiles. The 21 colors in this palette were selected not only for how they might coordinate with one another; they were also researched and tested for how they might be affected under various contemporary light sources. That is, "pink toned beiges allowed for the effects of fluorescent lighting, clean steel grays, and warm camels without the tendency 'to green.' "

The work of both Castelli and Walker/Group demonstrates how the contemporary use of color in textiles is approached as much as a science as a decorating tool. Larsen, however, also points out how the actual applications of textiles have changed in recent years. "Furnishings must compensate for indoor living in cities by providing organic rhythms, shade and shadow, lively surfaces, fiber itself. Fabrics must maximize light, provide privacy, and enhance a view," he says. "Also, the inherent acoustical and insulating properties of fiber are at last being rediscovered."

What Larsen is pointing out is the growing tendency to use textiles almost as an architectural element. Particularly in cramped urban spaces, visual privacy and separation can often be better achieved by a screen or panel than by constructing a new wall. Acoustical privacy can be accomplished with fabrics as well. Or, as lofts serve as residences more and more in urban areas, their occupants continue to discover how textiles, both as decorative and partitioning devices, are economical and efficient ways to introduce color and texture to expansive interior spaces. Textiles are not merely ornamental, but more and more serve the practical functions traditionally performed by more structural and permanent devices. As Larsen established, "The fabric of floors, walls, windows, and furniture covers will be the means to achieve variation in scale and pattern, color and texture."

The use of materials in textiles appears to be governed by a sense of integrity. That is, while the appeal of natural materials—linens, silks, cottons, and wools—that blossomed in the 1960s remains strong, so too does the appeal of synthetic materials. Yet the latter are used now less to represent another material; synthetic fibers are recognized for their own aesthetics rather than strictly for their imitative capacities. Similarly, contemporary textiles are likely to combine these synthetic fibers with natural fibers in compositions in which each offsets or dramatizes the other. Add this element to the pattern that has reappeared—to the pastel shades of the post modern color palette, to the coordinated color programs found increasingly in interiors, and to the use of fabrics and textiles as architectural devices—and it is evident that this is an area of vigorous and innovative design.

Product: Fret
Designer: Michael Graves
Princeton, New Jersey
Client: Sunar/Hauserman
New York, New York
Materials: 100 percent cotton

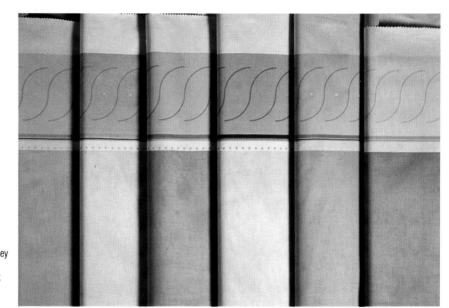

Product: Scroll
Designer: Michael Graves
Princeton, New Jersey
Client: Sunar/Hauserman
New York, New York
Materials: 100 percent cotton

Product: Tracery
Designer: Michael Graves
Princeton, New Jersey
Client: Sunar/Hauserman
New York, New York
Materials: 100 percent cotton

Product: California
Designer: Nathalie du Pasquier
            Paris, France
Client: Memphis
            Milan, Italy
Materials: Wool carpet, handwoven

Product: Isadora™
Designer: Gretchen Bellinger
            New York, New York
Client: Gretchen Bellinger
            New York, New York
Awards: 1981 Roscoe Award
Materials: Pleated silk

Product: Valkea Yo
Designer: Fujiwo Ishimoto
            Helsinki, Finland
Client: Marimekko Oy
            Helsinki, Finland
Awards: 1983 Roscoe Product Design award
Materials: 100 percent cotton

Product: Mirage Series
Designer: Staff design
Client: DesignTex
             Woodside, New York
Awards: 1983 IBD Product Design gold award
Materials: 51 percent linen, 49 percent rayon

Product: Kinnasand Collection
Designer: Staff design
Client: DesignTex
             Woodside, New York
Awards: 1982 ASID International Product Design
             award
             1982 IBD Product Design honorable
             mention
Materials: 100 percent cotton

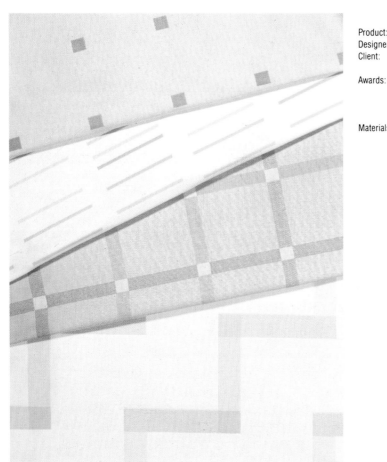

Products: (L to R) Sundown II, agate; Diamond
 Jubilee, silverweed; County Downs,
 straw; Limerick, meadow; Ribcord,
 moonstone; Merrion Square, silverweed;
 County Check, straw (front and back
 sides).
Design Firm: Jack Lenor Larsen design studios
 New York, New York
Client: Jack Lenor Larsen
 New York, New York
Materials: Sundown II, 100 percent wool; Diamond
 Jubilee, 100 percent wool; County
 Downs, 56 percent wool and 44 percent
 cotton chenille; Limerick, 100 percent
 wool; Ribcord, 50 percent worsted wool
 and 50 percent cotton; Merrion square,
 100 percent worsted wool; County
 Check, 57 percent wool and 43 percent
 cotton chenille

Product: Silhouette
Designer: Staff design
Client: DesignTex
 Woodside, New York
Awards: 1982 IBD Product Design silver award
Materials: 54 percent cotton, 46 percent polyester

Product: Coordinated Resources Program
Design Firm: The Walker/Group
 New York, New York
Materials: Fabrics, laminates, carpets, and ceramic
 tile for coordinated interior program.

Product: Prestwick Cloth
Designer: Ward Bennett
              New York, New York
Client: Ward Bennett Designs for Brickel
              Associates
              New York, New York
Materials: 70 percent wool, 30 percent nylon
              (acrylic backing)

Product: Unique Cloth
Designer: Ward Bennett
              New York, New York
Client: Ward Bennett Designs for Brickel
              Associates
              New York, New York
Materials: 100 percent cotton chenille

Product: Tapestry Cloth
Designer: Ward Bennett
              New York, New York
Client: Ward Bennett Designs for Brickel
              Associates
              New York, New York
Materials: 90 percent wool, 10 percent nylon
              Jacquard weave

Product: Waffle Weave
Designer: Ward Bennett
Client: Ward Bennett Designs for Brickel
              Associates
              New York, New York
Materials: 100 percent English worsted wool

Product:	Monochrome Range of Curtaining
Designer:	L. Davison, C. Kuhn
	Mowbray, South Africa
Client:	Sun Fabrics
	Mowbray, South Africa
Awards:	1982 Shell Consumer Product Design
	Award
Materials:	100 percent cotton, hand printed

Product:	Jhane Barnes Collection
Designer:	Jhane Barnes
	New York, New York
Client:	Knoll International
	New York, New York
Awards:	1983 ASID International Product Design
	award
Materials:	Lightweight cotton, wool, and rayon

Product:	Diamond Dancer
Design Firm:	Day & Ernst for Patterson, Flynn &
	Martin
	New York, New York
Client:	Patterson, Flynn & Martin
	New York, New York
Awards:	1983 Roscoe Product Design award
Materials:	Handpainted sisal rug

Designs for the Handicapped

In the discussion of contemporary product design, what is perhaps most compelling about design for the handicapped is that it has finally become a distinct and separate category in itself. Until recently, design for the handicapped referred largely to furniture that had been retrofitted for the impaired, or equipment whose highly clinical appearance, although it might accommodate a physical handicap, did little to psychologically accommodate the user. This is no longer the case. Take, for example, the walker designed for children made by Habermaass of West Germany. Until recently, most walkers had been aluminum. This one, however, is wood and has been painted bright red. It also has an attachment for a toy wagon. These new amenities help to remove the clinical stigma from the product, make it less intimidating to the child, and encourage its use.

Perhaps one reason that design for the handicapped has remained such uncharted territory is that standard anthropometrics rarely apply to the infirm. Designers who address the handicapped must frequently conduct their own research. In designing bathing fixtures for the handicapped, for example, Pascal Malassigne and James Bostrum discovered that, generally speaking, the size of people in the handicapped group they worked with was smaller than able-bodied subjects. The grants and financial support necessary to conduct the research that yields this information is not often so readily available to designers. That research information was available in this case, and that the new information was reflected in the design of the fixtures is not only encouraging; it also suggests that careful human factors research is likely to become and remain an integral part of designing for the handicapped.

Yet despite the fact that designers and critics have recognized design for the handicapped as an area that pleads for attention, products designed especially for the handicapped are not the only answers to the problem. More often, products designed for the able-bodied can accommodate the handicapped user as well. This, perhaps, is even more reassuring than the whole range of new products for the handicapped, simply because it demonstrates a more human approach. That is, disabilities can be accommodated by good design; they do not necessarily signal an abnormal condition that demands unique measures. The use of color, for example, is one simple way to answer certain needs of the elderly. The fading eyesight which often accompanies old age tends to make it difficult to distinguish the cooler colors, and diminishes perception of color intensity. Many colors look gray. Studies have indicated, not surprisingly, that the elderly often prefer more intense colors than do young people. Therefore, the increased use of bright colors in product and package design, while answering to a more general contemporary appetite for color and ornamentation, might also answer to this specific need of the elderly.

Victor Papanek states in his book *Design for Human Scale*, "Design is to technology what ecology is to biology." Nowhere does this become more evident than in design for the handicapped. To begin with, the term "handicapped" has a loose definition; it includes not only those with permanent disabilities, but can refer to the temporarily infirm, pregnant women, people under five feet tall perhaps, and quite often the elderly, who represent an increasingly important market as the population grows older. In other words, almost all of us, at some point or another in our lives, may be "handicapped." Although this may seem obvious, it has only recently been recognized and addressed as such.

Contemporary design for the handicapped also recognizes, finally, ergonomics. Because products and furnishings for the handicapped may be the areas that most need ergonomic design, it is ironic that they have been so long without it. As Bill Bash, designer of the Titann wheelchair, points out, most wheelchairs "though designed to sit in all day, are no more comfortable than your average church pew." The Titann wheelchair that he subsequently designed considers weight, portability, comfort, and durability. It is also narrower than standard wheelchairs and is foldable, permitting more convenient travel—and thus independence—for its user. Finally, the center of gravity on the chair is adjustable, allowing people of different height, build, and body structure to be comfortable in it.

Designers at Douglass Ball, Inc., in Canada have also addressed the transportation problem of wheelchair users. Their wheelchair restraint system designed for trains, buses, and specialized vehicles can adjust to a different number of wheelchair models. Telescoping arms fasten and lock the wheelchair into position against the wall, and a three-point belt system secures the passenger in his seat. Likewise, an elevator system designed by Douglass Ball recognizes "the fear, feelings of insecurity, frustration, and helplessness" of wheelchair users and the semiambulatory when boarding a bus, and was designed to allow passengers "to board in a dignified manner with movements of the elevator they are familiar with."

As all of these products demonstrate, user independence is the first objective in many of these designs. And whether they allow handicapped persons to drive, bathe, walk, or wheel themselves about more easily and comfortably, they are products that not only accommodate disabilities, but permit and encourage user independence and autonomy despite them. This shift in emphasis, too, distinguishes contemporary design for the handicapped.

Occasionally, and the occasions are certainly atypical, products designed for the handicapped, though intending only to afford greater comfort and independence, achieve even more substantial results. The ORLAU Swivel Walker is a case in point. The walker is designed to enable patients who are totally paralyzed from the waist down to walk. Although the walker can certainly be used by full-grown adults, its rewards are greatest when it is used by children at the age of 15 months and upward. As the walker's client—an English orthopedic hospital—maintains, the walker "provides ambulation which matches the normal development pattern. It is also beneficial in putting mechanical stress through the skeleton, thus substantially eliminating so-called spontaneous fractures which have so bedevilled ambulatory progress. And, the ability to be upright at an early age improves drainage of the urinary system, failure of which is a considerable potential danger." As great as (if not greater than) the comfort and independence allowed by the walker are its actual therapeutic advantages. The fact that products designed for the handicapped can have such therapeutic value places greater challenges—and gives greater rewards—to the industrial designer than those he might encounter designing more conventional products and furnishings.

Although it is not the case with the ORLAU Walker, a number of the products shown in this chapter are prototypes, rather than manufactured products which can be found on the market. They are included here, nevertheless, because design for the handicapped is an area so ripe for innovation and development that even prototypes, which may do nothing more than suggest new directions, are as important as those products already on the market.

Product: EVAC + Chair
Designer: David Egen
New York, New York
Design Firm: Egen Polymatic Corporation
New York, New York
Awards: 1982 IDSA Industrial Design Excellence
Award
1982 *Time* magazine selection for
"The Best of 1982"
Materials: Aluminum tubing; seat: vinyl covered
nylon pocket

Product: Foldable standard wheelchair
Designer: Jorg Ratzlaff and Frank Rieser
Hamburg, Federal Republic of Germany
Awards: 1983 Braun Prize for Technical Design

Product: IMP II Improved Mobility Package
               (This is for handicapped drivers for
               docking, transfer and retrieval, and
               storage.)
Designers: Joint design development between
               The Ford Motor Company
               Dearborn, Michigan
               and ASC Inc.
               Southgate, Michigan
Manufactured
and
installed by: Wisco Corporation
               Subsidiary of ASC Inc.
               Ferndale, Michigan
Materials: Power adjustable bench seat with integral
               padded transfer bridge; power wheelchair
               retriever and retaining system

Product: Electric curb-climbing wheelchair
               (This chair is equipped with small front
               wheel for indoor use.)
Design Firm: Douglass Ball Inc.
               Sainte-Anne-de-Bellevue, Quebec,
               Canada
Materials: Lightweight aluminum and steel

Product: Wheelchair restraint system for trains and buses
(This chair is equipped with adjustable head and backrest, three-point belt, and telescoping arms. The system is also designed for side-by-side installation and can also be converted into a special seat with pivoting armrest for semi-ambulatory passengers.)
Design Firm: Douglass Ball Inc.
Sainte-Anne-de-Bellevue, Quebec, Canada
Materials: Steel frame covered with ABS plastic

Product: Child's walker
Designer: Horst Dwinger
Rodach, West Germany
Client: Habermaass
Rodach, West Germany
Courtesy: The Able Child
New York, New York
Materials: Wood

Product: Titann Wheelchair
Designer: Bill Bash
               Lakeville, Minnesota
Client: Theradyne Corporation
               Lakeville, Minnesota
Materials: Black urethane spherical castor; titanium
               frame

Product: Chid's wheelchair
                (This chair comes with adjustable seat
                and back and armrest supports.)
Design Firm: Douglass Ball Inc.
                Sainte-Anne-de-Bellevue, Quebec,
                Canada
Materials: Molded foam; fabric; steel tubing

Product: Roll-In Shower
             (This is made for disabled people unable
             to transfer safely from a wheelchair.)
Designers: James A. Bostrum and
             Pascal Malassigne
             Atlanta, Georgia
Project
Engineer: William Sevebeck
             Blacksburg, Virginia
Materials: Fiberglass shells; wood floor and ramp
             Grants from the National Institute of
             Handicapped Research, U.S. Department
             of Education, and the Office of
             Rehabilitation Research and
             Development, the Veterans
             Administration, made this project
             possible.

Product: ORLAU Swivel Walker
Designer: G. K. Rose and Engineering Team
Client: Orlau, The Orthopedic Hospital
             Owestry, Shropshire, England
Awards: 1981 Design Council award
Materials: Steel and aluminum

Product:	Transfer Tub Seat
Designers:	Ronald L. Mace and Nancy Hurley
	Raleigh, North Carolina
Design Firm:	Barrier Free Environments, Inc.
	Raleigh, North Carolina
Awards:	1983 *Industrial Design* magazine
	Design Review selection
Materials:	Seat and transfer board: cross-linked
	polyurethane; adjustable base and
	clamps: stainless steel; armrest: stainless
	steel tube padded with vinyl-coated foam
	pad

Product:	Co-driver vehicle control device
	(This is designed to allow persons with
	lower-body and lower-limb disabilities to
	drive an automatic transmission vehicle
	using hands only.)
Designer:	N. Cohen
	Linksfield, South Africa
Awards:	1982 Shell Design Consumer Product
	award
Materials:	Steel and aluminum

Product: Multigrip cutlery with handle system
(This system is for those with grasping
or arm movement difficulties.)
Client: Roehampton
London, England
Courtesy: The Able Child
New York, New York
Materials: Stainless steel and plastic

Product: Eat and Drink Cutlery
(This is designed for persons with poor
grip or impaired hand/arm mobility)
Design Firm: Ergonomi Design Gruppen AB
Client: RFSU Rehab, Stockholm, Sweden
Materials: Flatware: black polycarbonate handles
and stainless steel; wine glass with extra
broad foot: polycarbonate; plate with
raised-lip edge and rubber friction ring
to prevent sliding: white heat-resistant
melamine